INTRODUCTION TO THE PSYCHOANALYTIC THEORY OF THE LIBIDO

THIRD EDITION

Introduction to the Psychoanalytic Theory of the Libido

by
Richard Sterba, M. D.
Clinical Professor of Psychiatry
Medical College, Wayne State University

1968
Robert Brunner, Inc.

Published by Robert Brunner, Inc.
80 East 11th Street
New York, N.Y. 10003

Preface to the Third Edition

INTRODUCTION TO THE PSYCHOANALYTIC THEORY OF THE LIBIDO
was written 36 years ago. It was the result of my first teaching assign-
ment at the Vienna Psychoanalytic Institute. Although the structural
viewpoint had been introduced 9 years earlier by Sigmund Freud's *The
Ego and the Id* (1922), and the transformation-theory of anxiety had
been replaced by the signal-theory of anxiety 5 years earlier by Freud
in *Inhibition Symptom and Anxiety* (1926), the libidotheory still
dominated the psychoanalytic thinking at the time of my lectures.
The maturational sequence of the predominance of the primary erotogenic zones and the regression to fixation points therein were considered of paramount importance for the diagnostic and therapeutic
assessment of the neuroses. Analysis was predominantly Id-analysis.
However, under the influence of Wilhelm Reich's contributions to
the understanding of and therapeutic dealing with the resistances
which the Ego produces in its defense against the uncovering of the
Id, the technical interest shifted considerably toward the Ego, a move
which later received a tremendous impetus through Anna Freud's
book, *The Ego and the Mechanisms of Defense* (1936). Although
the Ego was never underestimated by Sigmund Freud, it had not received the thorough investigation which the discovery of the drives
and their unconscious influence on behavior demanded during the
first 26 years of psychoanalytic exploration. The vast field of the
unconscious, its contents and its mode of functioning, so foreign to
the ways of conscious reasoning, had first to be plowed and harvested
with the help of psychoanalytic investigation of innumerable dreams
and neurotic manifestations before the Ego, the agent who estab-
lishes repression and other methods of defense, could become the
object of psychoanalytic study. With Anna Freud's book on the defense mechanisms the interest in the Ego and its defensive functioning
became gradually predominant. The Egostudies of Heinz Hartmann,
Erik Erikson and Rapaport began to dominate psychoanalytic thinking. Their concepts on Egodevelopment, Egostructure and -function-
ing are invaluable contributions to the understanding of the Ego's role
in the multidimensional functional system to which Freud gave the
name "mental apparatus."

Modern psychoanalytic literature is filled with Egostudies and Egotheories; one cannot help gaining the impression that this intense interest in the Ego had led to a decrease of the interest in the Id and its mighty dynamic currents. I therefore was delighted when the publisher asked me to have the libidotheory book reprinted. It is given here in its original form, partly for historical reasons, partly because it demonstrates that Freud's description of the different manifestations of the libido, his tracing of the developmental lines of their appearance and the theoretical concepts which he built on his observations retain their validity to a great extent. The 1931 text also makes us aware how relatively little has been added since then to our knowledge of libidinal phenomena and their dynamic influence in normal and pathological behavior.

The familiarity with the libidinous dynamism of the Id is still a necessity for the analytic investigator and therapist. Even for the psychodynamic understanding of the structure and the functioning of the Ego a knowledge of the libidotheory is indispensable. The phenomenon of the libidinous cathexis of the self-representation, which we call narcissism; the Ego's modes of functioning in continuation of early infantile libidinous activities connected with the dominant erotogenic zones; the phenomena of identification based on libidinous object relationships or their loss are a few cases in point—the theory of sublimation is based on it. We easily forget that Ego and Id are only gradually separated out of the common matrix of an undifferentiated state and that the Ego's structure and its most important functions—cohesion, integration and synthesis—are based on libidinous forces. Character traits are not only defensive, as Wilhelm Reich postulated, but fulfill also and often simultaneously libidinous demands determined by the forces of the Id.

The powerful energy sources of the mind are what in this book are called the "instincts." This was the original English term for the German "Trieb." Nowadays the term for the German "Trieb" is "drive" or "instinctual drive." The term "instinct" should be reserved for the instinctive reactions of animals, these innately given responses to specific stimuli coming from the surroundings. Animal "instincts" guarantee survival under the average condition of the biological niche in which the animal belongs. These are rigidly fixated in the genes and lead to automatic functioning when set in motion by the specific stimulus. Biologists also call them "innate release mechanisms" (IRM). In contrast to these functions which run their prescribed course automatically when the specific stimulus is perceived by the animal, the drives of the human being are characterized by their plasticity which enables them to some extent to be satisfied by substitute aims and objects. One of their essential features is transformability. To this the Ego owes a great part of its strength. The therapeutic aim, "Where Id was, there shall Ego be" (Freud, *New Introductory Lectures on Psychoanalysis*), can find realization due to the capacity of Id-drives to be absorbed by the Ego and transformed into dynamisms of creative productivity, thinking power and even defense structures against other Id-drives which have to be kept in repression.

The term "drive" for "Trieb" necessitates the change of the translation of the German term "Drang" designating the dynamic factor of the drive. The first English term for "Drang" was "drive." But "drive" we use now for the German "Trieb." We therefore have to use a new term for the "Drang" of the instinctual drive. The term "pressure" for the German "Drang" seems to me the most appropriate.

The dynamic aspect of the drive leads us to a discussion of the concept of "mental energy" which, following Freud's example, is extensively used in this book. The concept of mental energy has become controversial in recent years. It was created and used in psychoanalysis in analogy to the concept of energy in the physical world. Sigmund Freud wrote about such concepts in *Instincts and Their Vicissitudes*: "We have often heard it maintained that sciences should be built up on clear and sharply defined basic concepts. In actual fact no science, not even the most exact, begins with such definitions. The true beginning of scientific activity consists rather in describing phenomena and then in proceeding to group, classify and correlate them. Even at the stage of description it is not possible to avoid applying certain abstract ideas to the material in hand, ideas derived from somewhere or other but certainly not from the new observations alone. Such ideas—which will later become the basic concepts of the science—are still more indispensable as the material is further worked over. They must at first necessarily possess some degree of indefiniteness; there can be no question of any clear delimitation of their content. So long as they remain in this condition, we come to an understanding about their meaning by making repeated references to the material of observation from which they

vii

appear to have been derived, but upon which, in fact, they have been imposed. Thus, strictly speaking, they are in the nature of conventions—although everything depends on their not being arbitrarily chosen but determined by their having significant relations to the empirical material, relations that we seem to sense before we can clearly recognize and demonstrate them. It is only after more thorough investigation of the field of observation that we are able to formulate its basic scientific concepts with increased precision, and progressively so to modify them that they become serviceable and consistent over a wide area. Then, indeed, the time may have come to confine them in definitions. The advance of knowledge, however, does not tolerate any rigidity even in definitions. Physics furnishes an excellent illustration of the way in which even 'basic concepts' that have been established in the form of definitions are constantly being altered in their content."

Our understanding of psychic dynamic occurrences is greatly helped if we use the conceptual tool of "mental energy." The phenomena of augmentation, decrease through discharge, displacement, the mustering of defensive counterforces against strong dynamic drive currents which demand immediate gratification and many other dynamic occurrences in the psyche are brought to a better understanding if we use the analogical model of mental energy. We have to keep in mind, however, that we cannot equate mental with physical energy. Mental energy cannot be defined in terms of mass and acceleration, it is not based on elementary mass movements, it cannot be measured and quantified in an exact manner. We cannot even tie up psychic energy distinctly with the somatic processes in the neurons. And still at present no other concept than this one established in analogy to physical energy is as useful for the dynamic understanding of psychic processes. It gives us the best basis for our empathy into the processes in another's mind. I think that this is understandable if we follow the development of the concept of energy genetically.

The primeval and primitive understanding of the dynamic processes in our surrounding physical world is brought about by anthropomorphic projection. Primitive man, or the young child, in his first attempts to grasp what occurs in the physical world, considers the physical processes in the surroundings to be set in motion by forces equivalent to the dynamic processes of which he becomes aware in himself. In this early animistic world concept, nothing occurs that is not equal to the processes which he himself sets in motion or feels are set in motion in himself. The first dynamic world picture is a motivational one created through projection of the primitive's, or the child's, intrapsychic awareness of the motivational pressures within himself. Thus the concept of physical energy was in the beginning of human world-conception a projection of the psychic dynamic processes which were proprioceived. Physical energy is therefore an anthropomorphic concept. As science progressed, the necessity of making the concept of physical energy a useful one demanded that it be stripped of its anthropomorphic features. However, there can be no question but that it is legitimate to use the concept in its original primitive form in attempting to understand the dynamic occurrences in the mind. Nowhere is an anthropomorphic concept applied with more justification than in its place of origin, in "anthropos," i.e., with man. But it is inappropriate to demand that the properties which with the progress of science had to be attributed to physical energy in order to make the concept useful for the explanation of the phenomena of the physical world should be equally applied to "psychic energy." Psychic energy is a concept that corresponds to our immediate awareness of the dynamic processes within our mind. The expressions of everyday language which we use when we relate to psychic dynamic occurrences betray the underlying concept of psychic energy. "To feel driven by an irresistible power," "to exhaust one's energy fighting it," "to feel new strength" and many other expressions demonstrate this. Therefore we find it justified to continue to work with the conceptual tool "mental energy," ever ready to replace it if somebody offers a better one. Until then, we will consider "Libido" the term for "Sexual energy."

CONTENTS

INTRODUCTION TO THE
PSYCHOANALYTIC THEORY OF THE
LIBIDO

CHAPTER ONE

THE INSTINCTS

If we look for the English translation of the word "Libido" in a Latin dictionary, we shall find the words, desire, inclination, will, longing, appetite, passion. Cicero speaks of "ulciscendi libido" in the sense of "desire for revenge"; Tacitus of "Sanguinius libido", for bloodthirst, but the Church in the middle ages emphasized the erotic significance of the word, as in "oscula libidinosa", erotic kisses. Psychoanalysis, however, uses the term libido exclusively in connection with sexual pleasure and sexual desire. Freud has taken over this sense of the term from A. Moll, who makes use of it to designate the dynamic expression of sexuality. The manifestations of sexuality in human actions, dealings, thoughts and perceptions are considered to be the expression of a certain force or power (Greek: dynamis), and it is this force which psychoanalysis calls libido. We therefore speak of libido as the *dynamic energy of the sexual instinct*, or the energy which is expressed in the manifestations of the sexual instinct. This definition necessitates an explanation, first, of what an *instinct* is, and secondly, of the significance of the term *sexual*.

We will begin with the definition of the term *instinct*. The psyche has, with human beings as well as with animals, the task of mastering stimuli, of controlling them by means of the reactions with which it responds to these stimuli. Stimuli enter the psychic apparatus as a result of the energetic processes occurring in the outside world. Light, radiant warmth or the lack of it, sounds, change of position through active or passive movement, the impermeability of bodies, briefly, the entire physical surroundings are a continuous source of such stimuli. Our psychic surroundings too, our relatives, friends, colleagues, chance acquaintances and enemies are instrumental in the fact that our psychic life is never devoid of an incessant stream of stimuli and excitation. There are however also stimuli coming from within ourselves. These have their origin in somatic processes, in the

3

chemico-physical changes in the various organs and are called somatic stimuli or instincts. The difference between somatic stimuli and stimuli from outside is that we cannot withdraw from the somatic through flight; we carry the source of somatic stimuli within us and so can never escape them. Generally speaking, outside stimuli have the effect of a single blow, or perhaps rather of a series of single blows, whilst certain inner somatic stimuli are, on the other hand, characterized by their manner of flowing uninterruptedly into the psychic organ.

The instinct or impulse is the psychic representative of a continuously active stimulus originating in the interior of the body and flowing into the psyche from the somatic field. We think of the instinct as a psychic cause, in the form of a dynamic influence, for the mental manifestations which are observed in connection with this flowing in of somatic stimuli. Instincts are therefore intense psychic motions which, although they are physically felt and experienced, derive from somatic sources. Thus the term instinct is a borderline term, between the psychic and somatic; it represents the organic stimuli in the psyche as a dynamic factor. If we take as an example of organic stimuli the chemico-physical changes brought about by lack of nourishment, we will find that psychic manifestations result from the streams of excitation in the form of actions, specific sensations, changes of mood and so on. We regard as psychic the force which causes the mental manifestations of hunger, although its roots are in the somatic. We call this force the nutritional instinct. In the psychoanalytic sense the term instinct is an attempt to unify soma and psyche, or body and mind, which psychology has for centuries attempted to separate. Freud, with his concept of the instinct, tried to establish psychology on a biological basis and to abolish the artificial separation between soma and psyche.

As we have specified what we understand by the term instinct we can now investigate the characteristics by which one instinct can be distinguished from another. In the first place, there is the dynamic factor in the instinct, that is, the quantity of energy which it represents. We call this dynamic factor the *drive*, since we feel driven by a powerful instinct to actions and emotional reactions. We can estimate the driving power of the instinct by observing the degree of the hindrances it is able to surmount. In the case of hunger, when the instinctual drive is slight, gratification may easily be postponed by outside hindrances. On the other hand, when the drive of hunger is intense, the instinct makes urgent demands that the organ stimulus be removed, the limitations imposed by disgust may then be overcome and, in extreme cases of starvation, inhibitions are dissolved and objects which have hitherto been rejected or abhorred are used to satisfy hunger. The power of the instinctual drive may also be estimated by the quantity of hindrances or inhibitions the individual has to establish for himself in order to avoid a dangerous instinctual satisfaction.

A second characteristic of the instinct is its *aim*. The aim of the instinct is to re-establish a state in which there is no longer an instinctual need. This is naturally a very general definition of the aim of the instinct, because in the case of each individual instinct the removal of the state of stimulation at the instinctual source takes place by different means; with thirst it is otherwise than with hunger and with each individual component of the sexual instinct removal of stimulus is brought about by different means.

One general statement can be made about the attainment of instinctual aims, namely, that the decrease of instinctual tension through satisfaction is experienced by consciousness as pleasurable. This pleasurable experience of decrease in tension is however, like every experience, bound up with the psychic organization whose essential function is consciousness. The site of consciousness is the Ego. If the Ego, for reasons which we have yet to learn, opposes the satisfaction of an instinct, whilst the instinct, in spite of the Ego's objection, is able, owing to its strength, to enforce its satisfaction on the conscious personality, the conscious personality will react to this instinctual gratification with pain, unpleasure or anxiety. The Ego then suffers instead of getting pleasure through the instinctual satisfaction. This is what happens in the case of the neurotic symptom. Psychoanalysis finds that at the basis of every neurotic symptom there is an instinctual satisfaction which, in spite of the objections on the part of the conscious personality, achieves its aim but which, because of the disapproval of the Ego, is experienced as suffering, that is, as pain, or "unpleasure". The term "unpleasure" has been created as a parallel to the German term "Unlust", meaning the reverse of pleasure. The greatest instinctual pleasure which is experienced by healthy adults is that obtained through the union of the sexes in the sexual act.

As a third characteristic of the instinct, we must consider the *object*. The object of the instinct is easy to define. It is something belonging to the outside world by which or through which the instinct reaches its satisfaction. Usually we have the erroneous impression that there is always a close connection between the instinct and its object. Apart from the fact that there are instincts which find their satisfaction on the individual's own body, that is, without an outside object, the bond between instinct and object is not a primal one in the sense that the object arouses the instinct; it is the instinct which is primal and prior to the object and the connection with the object can only come about through the fact that it is considered appropriate for the attainment of satisfaction. The object is therefore the most variable characteristic of the instinct; it is, in the norm, easily transferrable in the domain of sexuality, and sometimes even in that of self-preservation. The slightness of the attachment to a specific food in the case of the nutritional instinct, where there is great hunger, will demonstrate the looseness of the bond between instinct and specific object. When an instinct is pathologically tied to a specific object, we speak of *fixation*.

The fourth and last characteristic of the instinct is its *source*. The instinctual source is that process in a somatic organ whose stimulus is represented in the psyche by the instinct. We must assume such a source of stimuli to exist in the case of each instinct, even if with few instincts we know the exact changes in the organs which represent for us the sources of excitation. The conditions of excitation, in the organs which have to be considered as instinctual sources, were formerly regarded in too simple a light by science in general. It was thought, for instance, that the lack of food content in the stomach led to the acids of the stomach beginning the work of digestion on the mucous membrane of the stomach itself. This conception proved false, because even persons who have been deprived of their stomachs through a surgical operation produce the sensations of hunger and the instinctual manifestations of these. Krafft-Ebing, the German psychiatrist, who was the first to describe systematically the sexual variations, considered as an instinctual source of the sexual instinct the overfilling of the spermatocyst with sperm, or better, the effect of the pressure brought about by the overfilling on the mucous membrane of the spermatocyst, a conception which could only be valid in the case of adult male sexuality. Actually however, the sources of our instincts are very much more complicated processes of a predominantly chemical nature. Our knowledge about the chemical constitution of these complicated processes is as yet most incomplete, since the fact that they take place inside our bodies in the form of chemical changes makes an exact examination extremely difficult. There is nevertheless hope that in the distant future the chemical instinctual sources will become known to us and then their composition can be thoroughly examined. The benefit of this knowledge in the case of neurosis, the cause of which, according to psychoanalytic findings, is traceable to instinctual processes, will be incalculable.

Now that the individual characteristics of the instinct have been explained, it will be helpful to demonstrate these by means of an example of a physical need which is an expression of the instinct of self-preservation, namely, the need to empty the bladder when it is full. The source of this need will at once be plain to us. It lies in the pressure exerted by the liquid in the bladder on the nerve ends of the mucous membrance of the bladder, and in the tension which the membrane experiences through the dilatation caused by the bladder being filled with urine.[1] This is the source, that is to say, the condition of organ excitation which is represented in the mind as a need or an in-

---

[1] In pathological cases, other causes such as stimulus through inflammation can produce the same urge, even when the bladder is empty.

stinct. We called the motive power of such a process the *drive* of the instinct, and we can measure the drive by the amount of hindrances which can be overcome in order that the instinct may obtain satisfaction. If the pressure in the bladder is very great, a person may be compelled to overcome the sense of shame and to empty it in unusual circumstances. We can well imagine in the case of bladder pressure that there is a direct relationship between the amount of organ excitation and the drive of the instinct. The greater the quantity of urine and the greater the pressure and tension in the bladder, the more intense the organ excitation will be and, accordingly, so much the greater will be the drive of the instinctual need and the readiness to overcome hindrances in the way of gratification.

We defined as the *aim* of the instinct the satisfaction, that is to say, the removal of the condition of excitation at the somatic instinctual source. The gratification, in our example of the urinary need, is the emptying of the bladder, which leads to the removal of the tension and pressure that the mucous had to endure; it signifies, therefore, the re-establishment of a condition in which the need of the instinct has been removed. We know that the satisfaction of the urinary need, through the emptying of the bladder, is a pleasurable experience and that it is the more pleasurable the greater the pressure—that is, the more intense the stimulus which was carried from the source of the instinctual need to the psychic apparatus. We termed the *object* of the instinct any outside object able to bring about instinctual satisfaction; in the case of the urinary need, the object is the place where the bladder can be emptied. The exchangeability of the object and its slight connection with the instinct is particularly noticeable in our example. It will also be evident that it is not the instinct which is aroused by the object, but the object which is sought out by the driving instinct.[2]

It is possible with a person deprived of consciousness for the

---

[2] In the case of the urinary need, the distinction between the characteristics of the instinct is so obvious that there will be no need of a more elaborate description of the process of urinary gratification which, to some extent, causes an auto-erotic satisfaction too and in which the urine itself has to be considered as an object of instinctual satisfaction.

bladder, when full, to empty itself spontaneously, without participation of the psychic organ. We call this short-circuit a *reflex action*. When this reflex action occurs, the stimulus flows from the stimulated organ over the spinal cord and lower brain centres, without taking the roundabout way over the grey matter—the seat of consciousness—back to the muscular apparatus of the bladder; the latter reacts by exerting muscular contraction which leads to the emptying of the bladder. We cannot count this reflex among the instinctual processes, because instinctual processes are those in which the psyche participates. It is only when the route over the grey matter and therefore over the psyche is taken that we consider the process as instinctual. For the instinct is the mental and mentally experienced cause of the mental manifestations upon the organ stimulus. The emission of urine by an individual deprived of consciousness is the reflex action to a stimulus. Only the mental actions which, owing to urinary pressure, lead to the emptying of the bladder, can be called instinctual manifestations. These actions are accompanied and influenced by innumerable other psychic processes which shape, inhibit or increase them. The participation of the psyche is an essential condition in those processes which we call instinctual, since the term instinct, in psychoanalysis, unites the mental with the somatic field.

We have already learnt that the psychic apparatus serves to control the stimuli; we saw that many stimuli enter the psyche from the outside world, but they also pour in in a continuous stream from the interior of the body, in the form of instinctual or organ-stimuli. These instinctual stimuli play a most important part in the mental life. The psychic organ has in general one aim—to be at peace or to reach the condition of being at peace. The stimuli which flow into it disturb this peace and adequate measures must be taken to remove them, so that the condition of peace may be regained. This recovery of peace is termed restoring control of the stimuli. However, the outside world and the subjection of the psychic life to our bodies, or better, the union which the body and the psyche represent, prevent the complete condition of peace striven for by the psyche being realized before death. An incessant counter-play of forces is the fundamental basis of the psychic process. Why do we use the expression "counter-play of forces"? Because the changes in the outside world bring constantly changing stimuli and because within the instincts themselves antagonistic tendencies are manifested. In many cases, the instinctual tendencies from within oppose the efforts of the psyche to restore control of the stimuli coming from the outside world, so that the instinctual satisfaction has to be prohibited or postponed or the instinctual aim has to be changed.

Freud has taught us to consider two large groups of instincts as fundamentally antagonistic, namely, the instinct of self-preservation and the sexual instinct. Later to some extent, he abandoned this conception of antagonistic instincts, but we will go over it in detail nevertheless and will give the reasons leading to the establishment of the dualism of the instinct of sexuality and self-preservation, because this conception will best enable us to understand the psychic counter-play of forces. As Freud's first dualistic principle, it is certainly worth studying from the standpoint of the historical development of psychoanalysis, and it is indispensable for the clinical and practical comprehension of most psychic, and particularly psychopathological, manifestations.

Popular opinion has already differentiated between the instincts of hunger and love and knows that they are antagonistic to each other. Hunger as the representative of the instinct of self-preservation is often either in open or secret conflict with love, in which instinct the sexuality of man seems to reach its culminating point. Even superficial observation will disclose the antagonism between the two groups of instincts which are represented by hunger and love. A violent love sometimes causes neglect of important functions of self-preservation and can be a menace to the welfare of the individual, even to the extent of endangering his existence, whilst on the other hand, love relations may suffer greatly through strong expression of the instinct of self-preservation. In such cases, we often see love ties destroyed.

Freud had another reason for contrasting the instincts of self-preservation and sexuality: if we examine the biological function of the individual, that is to say, the task he is here to fulfill, we find that it is two-fold. Man's first aim is to live as an individual, striving with all his might to maintain his existence, prolonging it to the utmost and guarding himself from danger. However, he does not only live as an individual, but also as a link in the concatenation of generations of his species and he has, in his character of a link in the chain, to do his duty by the species. As a sexual being too he has a task to fulfill which often threatens to destroy his existence. In the animal world the menacing significance of sexuality is frequently striking; in the case of the salmon, the fulfilment of the sexual functions costs him his life; the mountain cock abandons its amazing caution when in the grip of the sexual instinct, so that, while it is performing its dance of love, the hunter can almost touch it with his hand; the male spider, like the drone, pays for the sexual act by death. Mankind too is subjected to this dual biological function which, from the biological standpoint, justifies the concept of two antagonistic groups of instincts. This dualistic conception is established in accordance with the future possibility that we will be able to find a specific chemical basis for the sexual instincts at their source, by which they may be differentiated fundamentally from the instincts of self-preservation; the sexual instincts are, psychologically, essentially different from the Ego instincts in that they are far less controlled by the higher psychic activities. They tend towards the pathological, indeed are always such in their manifestations if the individual shows any variants in the domain of the psyche. They are frequently "abnormal" also in cases where the individual otherwise enjoys complete psychic health. They are wilful, cannot easily be influenced, are irrational and consequently are not easily accessible to education. They do not want to learn.

CHAPTER TWO

ON HUMAN SEXUALITY

Having differentiated between Ego instincts and sexual instincts we will try to evaluate the range of the sexual instinct.' By determining the compass of the sexual instinct and discovering the wealth of its manifestations, we shall also be able to answer the second question which arose from the definition of libido as sexual instinct energy, namely, what is the meaning of the term "sexual"? The answer was formulated in many different ways before Freud's investigations were made. One opinion, not only popular, but which also unfortunately frequently serves as a scientific basis, is that sexual matters are identified with the indecent. Our culture to a great extent had its origin in and was built upon the repression of the instincts. If, owing to their cultural education, people have a tendency to reject instinctual satisfaction, it is comprehensible, though not scientifically justifiable, that the attitude of their cultural institutions towards the sexual instincts will be hostile. This ethical and moral rejection of sexual instincts led to the identification of all that is sexual with the indecent. We cannot accept this definition because it is based on an evaluation which will prevent us from understanding the true nature and range of the sexual instinct. However, as far as our own individual affective evaluation is concerned, we do actually identify much of what is sexual with the indecent. Another definition, which is not based on emotional evaluation, determines as sexual all intentions which aim at gaining pleasure through the sexual organs of the opposite sex, in order to attain sexual union. This definition is of too limited a nature, as is the other which emphasizes propagation as the essential goal of sexuality, for there are a great number of sexual actions which do not aim at propagation, such as kissing, masturbation, or the innumerable perverse actions of men which must, judging by our own empathy, be characterized as sexual. It is better not to demand a strict definition of sexuality, bearing in mind instead what has been acknowledged and recognized as sexual through observations made from a strictly objective and scientific standpoint, as is being attempted by psychoanalysis. We shall see, in forming an opinion regarding those manifestations of human sexual life which psychoanalysis pronounces to be sexual, that there is no essential difference between most of these and what, according to our feelings, we consider to be sexual in the adult.

We will follow Freud's example and pass in review the perversions of mankind's sexual life. The varied spectacle of such a display will make it evident to us how wide are the delimitations of the sexual life of man. We shall see that it is not possible to shut out the perversions from the sexual life of human beings and a definition of sexuality must necessarily include them. The healthy sexual act, with its preparatory actions, falls naturally within the boundaries of sexuality and indeed, according to Freud, forms the systematizing principle in the classification of the perversions.

We will begin by enumerating these. First of all, we shall have to deal with those individuals for whom the opposite sex constitutes a hindrance to the satisfaction of the sexual instinct, who can only attain satisfaction with a member of the same sex. We call such individuals homosexual, or inverted. Their number is legion. In certain cultural epochs homosexuality was not outlawed and condemned, but admitted and even recommended, as for instance, with the ancient Greeks. In homosexuality, the deviation from health lies in the choice of the sexual object. Then there are perverse individuals with whom the sexual aim differs from that of the norm. They do not strive for sexual union of the genitalia, but obtain their greatest pleasure from other parts of their partners' bodies, from the hands, the hair, the feet, or the mouth. The interest of other perverse individuals is concentrated on the excretory functions of the desired object and they experience their pleasure in observing this function with the loved object. These two variations deviate from the healthy sexual aim of coitus with the partner, in that the sexual interest is transferred to neighboring or more remote regions of the partner's body, which procure them more intense pleasure than the genitalia themselves. The remoteness from the legitimate goal may be even more pronounced, as in the case of fetishism, in which the sexual object, although deriving from the partner, is separated from the original love object and equipped with the independent ability to give the most intense pleasure. Shoes, articles of clothing, garters, hair ribbons, procure for these people what is normally afforded by the genitalia of the partner. Others again demand astonishing conditions of the object; it must be crippled in some way, with only one leg, one arm, or some other defect, in order that they may experience it as a sexual object. The most extreme case of this kind is represented by those who attach the condition of being dead to the loved object, whether they seek out a corpse, as do the Necrophiles, or whether the loved object has to become a corpse, that is be killed at the moment of most intense satisfaction. We read often enough in the newspapers of such sex murders, but must reckon the number as being far greater of those who, in this domain, do not go further than wishing and producing fantasies of this kind, but must still be considered as perverse.

A large series of the perversions consists in the fact that the most intense pleasure is not obtained by the final act, but from the preparatory actions or from one such action. Looking at the object or rather at intimate parts of the body completes the pleasure-process for such perverse individuals; touching may also lead to this, or the act of undressing, as will all actions which, in the healthy approach of the sexes to the sexual act, play an important preparatory part in the emphasis and increase of pleasure. What we call perversion may be described partly as an arrest at the intermediate stage of the approach to the love act, partly as a violation of the boundaries intended by the physique for healthy sexual functions.

A large group of perverse individuals find pleasure not in tender but in cruel actions, in active or passive form, that is, in inflicting or suffering pain and grief. This pain can consist in physical mistreatment or can be limited to the psychic domain, manifesting itself in the form of humiliation, degradation, scorn, mental torture and so on. We call those who carry out cruel actions sadists and their suffering partners masochists. Usually in a perverse person both sadism and masochism are to be found, indeed perversions of the most diverse kind may be manifested in the same person.

Why do we have to include those countless, often horrifying aberrations which we call perversions, in the domain of human sexuality? Do they not belong far more to the domain of mental diseases and psychic variations of a severe kind? The number of perverse persons is very great and many of them are people who have otherwise mature, successful personalities. For instance, Jean Jacques Rousseau who, to a great extent, inspired the French Revolution by his writings, described his own masochistic fantasies, desires and practices in his Confessions. The famous composer, Tschaikowsky, was homosexual. From a scientific standpoint, the number of perverse people is considerable, since we must include among them not merely those practicing perversions, but also the far greater number who only do so in their fantasies. If the perversions are not included in our sexual investigations we shall certainly have to exclude half of mankind. Neuroses show us, in analysis, that the hidden content of a symptom is always a perverse tendency which the neurotic has forbidden himself. Therefore when we find signs of a neurotic symptom, we must assume the existence of unconscious perverse tendencies. The manifest content and particularly the hidden content of our dreams reveal desires for perverse satisfaction and their distorted fulfilment.

Perverse people merely carry out what others, and in a certain sense all of us dream and wish or, as will be explained, what all of us have once wished and done. And so, if the perversions are to be regarded as common to all mankind, they lose their horror to a great extent. They are characteristic features of mankind and are to be found in some degree in the most healthy people. In their sexual behavior, healthy grown-up persons show allusions to perversity, either feeling and expressing mild sadistic tendencies during the sexual act, or, in order to increase the pleasure by variation, violating the anatomical boundaries, using other regions than the genitals to obtain satisfaction.

Who then must we consider perverse in the strict sense of the term? Those for whom the perverse action—the deviation from the healthy union of the genitals—forms the predominant or exclusive satisfaction. This exclusivity is in the clinical sense the distinctive mark of the perverse individual, apart from which we can merely speak of deviations of a perverse character. However, in general, the terms "perversion", "perversity" or "perverse", are used interchangeably either for exclusive perversions or for occasional perverse deviations.

When we make the clinical diagnosis of "perversity", we mean we consider the individual to be perverse in the narrower sense of exclusivity. When however a perverse tendency is observed as the basis of a neurotic symptom, we do not call the otherwise healthy person suffering from this symptom perverse, we say instead that he has in him a perverse tendency.

It has been mentioned that the perverse person merely carries out what we have all once done or wished to do. What does this mean? We shall be able to understand this statement if we make up our minds to observe children very carefully, examining their behavior objectively. We shall then soon discover that there are a great many instinctual manifestations in the child where the evidence of sexuality cannot be disputed. The fact that children have sexuality is profoundly shocking to anyone hearing it for the first time; indeed he is likely to disbelieve it, owing to his inner attitude of resistance. There is a tendency in all adults to repress experiences, actions, thoughts and wishes belonging to their childhood, which education has obliged them to repress from memory. There is a tendency which makes us resist the recognition that children have sexuality, since to admit it as a fact would be to acknowledge that we ourselves had sexuality during childhood. The task undertaken by our cultural education, of obliterating the memory of the instinctual sexual tendencies of childhood involves much suffering and anxiety on the part of the child until it is accomplished; it is therefore comprehensible that the individual struggles with might and main against the abolition of this work. Once however resistance is thrust aside by means of an intellecutal, coolly objective judgment, or is removed by a personal psychoanalysis, the manifestations of sexuality in children can no longer be overlooked.

We have claimed that certain features of the child's behavior must be regarded as sexual. How can this be proved without defining what we consider as sexual? It is clear from our own knowledge and conviction that the perversions are sexual. We know this through empathy and from the testimony of perverse people who regard their perversion as their sexuality. If we find the same manifestations in the child, why should we not look on these as sexual? Only our own affective inner resistance can prevent us, because to do so would involve admitting our own infantile sexuality. However, if this resistance is removed, the surest method being through a personal psychoanalysis, we shall no longer be in doubt as to what is sexual in adult behavior or in that of the child; we shall recognize and feel what we have to assume as sexual manifestations in children. This knowledge gained through empathy will of course be of a subjective nature.

As an illustration of an infantile action considered by psychoanalysis to be sexual, we will take pleasure-sucking or thumb-sucking. A child sucks his thumb with his lips and tongue, without deriving any kind of benefit from the point of view of self-preservation.[3] In this infantile activity of thumb-sucking, details may be observed which are also manifested in the sexual activity of grown-up people. Pleasure-sucking is done rhythmically and most sexual activities of adults show the same rhythm. A curving course is to be perceived during the process of pleasure-sucking. It begins gently, grows more agitated, finally reaches a culminating point and then subsides. The sexual activities of adults follow the same course. The culminating point of pleasure sucking is sometimes accompanied by a general excitation which takes possession of the entire musculature. The orgasm (the maximum pleasure-experience and the most intense satisfaction

---

[3] One of the objections which has been raised by psychologists against these infantile pleasure actions being called sexual is that it has been said that they serve the purpose of training for subsequent Ego functions. The sucking movements of the mouth however are known by the child from the beginning of his existence, they are inherited reflex mechanisms and lose their importance at a later age.

an adult can feel in the sexual act) shows a similar general reaction. The most important point in common between thumb-sucking and the sexual manifestations of grown-up people, is the unquestionably pleasurable experience of both. Whoever has observed an infant's pleasure in thumb-sucking and the calm and quiet which possesses him at the end of this activity, will be compelled by this objective test of pleasure to recognize that, between thumb-sucking (an example taken from similar childhood habits) and the sexual activities of adults, there is a deep affinity. If you ask older children why they do it, they will answer: "Because it feels good!" Qualities which from the subjective as well as from the objective standpoint, characterize the sexual manifestations of adults, are also to be observed in these childish activities. It is therefore only logical to consider these too as sexual acts.

CHAPTER THREE

DESCRIPTION AND HISTORY OF THE DEVELOPMENT OF CHILD SEXUALITY

If the sexual manifestations of children are observed in their temporal sequence, we shall see that they make their appearance in a certain order. An intense sexual activity, taking place at a particular region of the body, will, after a certain period, be abandoned and replaced by sexual activity at another region of the body. Observations of many different children and analytical observations of the childhood memories of adults have proved that the changing sexual manifestations of the child follow one another in a typical sequence. Psychoanalysis regards this sequence as the manifestation of a development. The phases of this development are the oral (at the site of the mouth zone), the anal (anal zone), and the genital (zone of the sexual organs). Each of these stages can roughly be divided into two phases.

a. The First Oral Phase

The first sexual manifestation of the child begins soon after birth, when it starts to try to obtain pleasure at the zone of the mouth. When a baby is spared the act of birth by a Caesarian operation, the child is often revealed lying in the uterus, with a finger in its mouth, sucking it in these most peaceful of all surroundings. Sometimes children are born with a thumb ulcerated from intrauterine sucking. The ancient Egyptians represented their God Horus as a new-born child sucking his finger. What is pleasure-sucking? It is a rhythmical sucking of the mucous membrane of the mouth with the tongue, with a finger, a toe or any other part of the skin, even with an object. The entire attention of the child is absorbed by this pleasure-sucking; at the climax of the activity a stretching of the whole body is sometimes to be observed, which is very similar to what occurs with an orgasm. Frequently pleasure-sucking is combined with the child's rubbing some part of the body with the hand—often the lobe of his ear, sometimes the genitals. In this way, his attention may be directed to what becomes later the central zone of his sexuality. The discovery of the genitals as dispensers of pleasure accompanying that of pleasure-sucking, can lead to the independent rhythmic rubbing of the genitals, which we often notice even with sucklings and which we call suckling-masturbation.[4]

We have differentiated between the characteristics common to all instincts, and have demonstrated these in the example of

---

[4] Before Freud emphasized the sexual character of thumb-sucking, S. Lindner, a Hungarian pediatrician recognized it as an erotic activity of infants and children. He described it as such but, according to the prevailing attitude of the time, attempted to deny the sexual character of this activity. Among other careful observations he states:

". . . Since however the reasons for pleasure-sucking which have been cited do not inspire us with great confidence, we must assume that in every child there is an inherent disposition to pleasure-sucking, which under given circumstances, can lead to a state of "sucking rapture."

". . . One frequently sees the pleasure-sucker at the stage of rapture with his head shaking up and down, his spine as in an emprosthotonous writhing forwards, his feet striking the ground or, if he is in a lying position, jerking. It is at this stage that he draws blood, tears things up or obstructs the organs of smell and of sound. If one speaks to the pleasure-sucker and asks him something at the height of his pleasure, he will not answer, at most he will nod or shake his head, for yes or no. If one disturbs him he will get up angrily and run away, without for one moment ceasing his pleasure-sucking, to look for a place where he will not be disturbed. Sometimes such children are so far lost to the world that they do not even notice threats and are deaf even to kind words.

"If the child is lying in bed he will eventually go to sleep, after the rapture has passed, with whatever he has been sucking in his mouth. The assisting hand falls in the position dictated by its own weight—if the arm does not happen to be bent over the head—so that it can return to its post when the child half wakes. . . .

". . . It is as difficult to wean children from pleasure-sucking as from the breast, since pleasure-sucking is a substitute for the breast.

". . . Among other things, my toe-sucking little girl patient says: 'Sucking is more fun than eating'. . . .

". . . I have no intention other than of stating a fact when I add that the pleasure-points with children which are stimulated during pleasure-sucking, are somewhat similar to the highest pleasure-points (puncta libidinosa) in adult erotic life. The difference is that in the sexual life of adults there is usually active assistance procured by means of another heterogeneous individual, only as an exceptional deviation alone (masturbation) or by means of another homogenous person (pederasty and lesbian love). Another distinction is that the fondling of the pleasure-points in adult love life has rather the significance of preparation than of accompaniment. . . ." Dr. S. Lindner, Budapest. Jahrbuch fuer Kinderheilkunde. 1879.

the need to urinate. We will now demonstrate them on the activity of pleasure-sucking, the first instinctual manifestation of a sexual nature. We found that the first characteristic of every instinct is its motive power, its drive. With the suckling, the intensity of the instinctual drive is shown by the strength of the desire, and the pleasure-value can therefore be rated by the frequency that pleasure-sucking is practised. The intensity of the pleasure-sucking is as it were a measure of the degree of the oral instinctual drive. We shall be able to see, in the following case, which I observed myself, an unusually high degree of this oral instinctual drive: A little girl of 4 sucked her thumbs so violently and incessantly that both became ulcerated; however in spite of this she tried throughout an entire night to free her thumbs from the bandages the doctor had put on them, and finally succeeded in getting at one of the ulcerated thumbs and sucking it. In this case, an unusually strong instinctual drive persisted long after the time when pleasure-sucking should have been given up.

The intensity of the drive may be estimated by the efforts made to overcome the obstacles to satisfaction. The degree of intensity of the instinctual drive is of great significance for the individual, because the greater the drive the more difficult it is to control its manifestations, to master the instinct. Human beings are forced to subdue a great part of their sexual drives, that is to say, the direct satisfaction of these instincts has to cease and their energies have to be used in another way. Our education and the culture and civilization to which we belong require this of us and it is necessary in order that we may be provided with additional energy for our life's task. How great is the hostility of adults towards relics of infantile instinctual gratifications can be demonstrated by means of two examples which, as a matter of fact, have nothing to do with the educational methods applied to the small child, but are taken from the attitudes of people towards domestic animals.

I had occasion once to watch a bull which would suck for hours at its own turned back tongue. The breeder had the bull slaughtered because he did not wish to breed from a beast with such a bad habit, although in every other respect it was perfect.

A well bred, fine-looking dog that would suck half the day at the upper part of his leg was thrown out as worthless by another breeder. We are still more severe about unnecessary instinctual gratifications when, as happens frequently, our own children cling to them beyond the tolerated period, for we wish to form our children according to models of our own ideals and of ourselves, by means of our education. Education necessitates the subjugation of the child's instincts and the greater the instinctual drive the more difficult the task.

How does it come about that the strength of the instinctual drive varies in different children? Two factors have to be considered as responsible in a strong instinctual drive. First, that of disposition or heredity. Every instinct is as we have seen founded on an organic basis. This organic basis we have to regard as inheritable. When a marked oral tendency, that is a strong instinctual disposition to eroticism of the mouth zone, is present in one or both parents, then whether this has made itself manifest in the parents or not, it is possible that the child through the double inheritance from the parents will have an abnormally strong organic basis which will manifest itself in intense instinctual drives of an oral nature.

Besides this inner factor of the inherited disposition, there is also a second outside factor to be taken into account, that of the surroundings. For instance, an irresponsible educator may encourage the child's oral instinctual satisfaction by giving him a rubber pacifier to quiet him. The child will then cling to this oral satisfaction until past the time when it should be replaced by others and the instinctual energy used for other purposes. An instinctual drive stronger than it should be for the child's age can be very harmful. An irrational mother will usually not succeed in curbing the instinctual drive because her own too strong identification with the child—through which she participates unconsciously in the child's pleasure—will prevent her from doing so. This can bring about a dangerous psychic situation since, eventually, the child has to give up sucking the pacifier or the thumb (the favorite objects for pleasure-sucking). If the full strength of the instinct is retained the ultimate renunciation will be extraordinarily hard; he will not be able to give up his desire for oral satisfaction, he will only be able to suppress it with great difficulty and in circumstances most unfavorable to himself; he may even be forced later on to allow the instinct a substitute satisfaction in the form of a neurotic symptom which he will have to endure against his will.[5]

The aim of the pleasure-sucking instinct is, as with all instinctual aims, satisfaction, that is, the removal of stimulus at the instinctual source. The removal of the stimulus is brought about by pleasure-sucking, that is, by the rhythmical sucking movement of the membrane of the mouth and the touching of the object. To desire satisfaction and to strive for the instinctual goal the child must already know what this gratification is, that is to say, he must once have experienced the process releasing this satisfaction. It is not difficult to discover what opportunity the suckling has had to enjoy pleasure-sucking for the first time. The mother's breast gives him his first sexual satisfaction, unless the inherited instinct for pleasure has not already led to the discovery of the possibilities of the mouth zone, as we may assume in the case of our intra-uterine pleasure-sucker.

A similar connection to that observed between the suckling's taking of nourishment and his sexual instinctual satisfaction is to be seen with all other infantile sexual pleasure activities. The sexual satisfactions of the child are experienced on those organs and zones which have an important function to accomplish in his self-preservation. Thus in infancy it is characteristic that sexual satisfaction takes place simultaneously with the self-preservative activity of these organs. It is these organs which, owing to their function of self-preservation, come into relationship with the outside world. The organs active as infantile sexual instinctual sources are those which attend to the ingestion of food and the ejection of excrements, the musculature which has to accomplish movement in the outside world, the senses, par-

---

[5] A too early suppression of the instinctual activity can, on the other hand, also cause lasting psychic damage, because there often remains an unquenchable longing for the forbidden satisfaction which makes the individual incapable of appreciating other gratifications. The child should therefore only be made to give up an instinctual satisfaction when one can offer him another in its place.

ticularly the eyes, and the skin with its sensibility to touch and feeling; all these play an important part in the self-preservation of the individual.

The sexual instinct detaches itself from the nutritional instinct very early and seeks its satisfaction independently; this is evident in the case of pleasure-sucking, since the suckling begins pleasure-sucking very early, regardless of his hunger being appeased. The fact that originally the sexual instinct and the somatic need were functionally connected can have disastrous results in certain cases of neurotic illnesses; a repression of oral sexual tendencies can, for instance, cause an inhibition of the self-preservative function of the mouth zone, that is, of eating. Thus the little girl who, as a four year old child still sucked with all her might at her sore thumb, suffered in later years from hysterical vomiting on every occasion involving her sexual feelings; this had a very serious effect on her health, causing a great loss of weight. In this case, the original connection between the two instinctual gratifications of self-preservation and sexuality led to an inhibition of the self-preservation instinct when sexual gratification at the oral zone was blocked.

Here, in order to form an opinion regarding the origin of our instinctual cravings, we shall have to supplement what we have already said about instincts. One necessary factor has already been determined, namely, the experience of satisfaction and the pleasure sensation which satisfaction has brought with it. Once having had a pleasure experience, it is clear that under given circumstances there will be a desire to re-experience it. Due to apparently organic reasons, which are chemically unknown to us, there then results in the mind a sensation of tension which is felt as pain or "unpleasure". This feeling of tension is, in the case of oral instinctual demands, projected to the mouth zone and experienced there as irritation or excitement. We cannot ask the suckling what experiences or sensations provoke him to pleasure-sucking, however we occasionally find relics of the infantile search for oral pleasure in adults who can give us information regarding their need for satisfaction at the oral zone. For instance, I was treating a man in analysis who, as a child, had been an immoderate pleasure-sucker and who, as an adult became a drunkard, continuing his oral pleasure-sucking in the form of drinking. He explained that an unpleasant feeling of tension around his lips and gums drove him to drinking. This was not thirst, but a desire for the activity and the sensations in the mouth zone produced by the act of drinking. The feeling of tension experienced by the suckling at the mouth zone is considered by psychoanalysis as similar to that in the example just cited.

The investigation of the instinctual aim and of its establishment after the child's first experience of activity at the oral zone during nutrition has also shown us the instinctual *sources* and their locality, i.e. the lips, the tongue, parts of the palate and the mucous membrane of the cheeks; we learnt too the kind of stimuli which these sources send into the psyche. Here, we shall have to explain the meaning of a new term. A region of the body, such as the mouth zone, which is able to send sexually exciting stimuli to the psyche, we call an erotogenic zone. The acquisition of libidinal "organ pleasure" is bound up with such erotogenic zones, of which there are very many distributed over the whole body. We will name them later. Some erotogenic zones are the sources of particularly intense sexual urges. The instinctual energies of these zones, that is, of the mouth, the anal and the genital zones, have a particular significance because of their subsequent development and their marked influence up till the time of maturity on the formation of the psyche. These prominent erotogenic zones are also able to some extent to seize and make use of the sexual excitation from other sources, augmenting in this way their own desire for satisfaction and sometimes thus attaining a certain domination over the remaining sources of sexual excitation. These erotogenic zones are called *primacy* zones and the subordination of the remaining instinctual sources to the primacy zone is termed libido organization. In following the historical order of infantile sexual activity we see that the different primacies succeed each other in a typical temporal order, the predominance of one primacy zone thus passing over to another. The different changes which manifest themselves in the psyche with the passing of the sexual primacy from one zone to another will be dealt with in the course of this history of the development of the libido.

During the suckling period, pleasure-sucking is not the only sexual activity. We assume that, even at this time, the emptying of the bladder and intestines does not occur without sexual excitation, that, above all, the passive rocking movements in the cradle or arms and being carried around arouse intense pleasure experiences in the child. We have already mentioned the suckling masturbation often noticeable in the form of a rubbing movement of the genitals. However, the most striking of the sexual gratifications at this early period is the activity of sucking, which we consider lasts from the first days of life until towards the end of the sixth month. We call this period the first oral phase of the child's libido development.[6] The predominance of the mouth zone remains throughout the following phase, but the form of the pleasure changes with the appearance of the teeth.

b. THE SECOND ORAL PHASE

The new form of sexual satisfaction at the mouth zone, which, with the use of the teeth replaces the activity of sucking and becomes the dominating sexual activity of the infant, consists in masticating and devouring. If one observes a child at this period, noticing the pleasure with which he puts things in his mouth and tries to destroy them with his teeth, how at a certain stage he attempts to chew up every attainable object and swallow it, one gets a clear idea of the pleasurable instinctual activity produced by the masticating apparatus. The immediate reaction of the child to an object which he likes at this age is to put it in his mouth and eat it. Even in grown-up language, we have a relic of this in the words "I could eat it", which we use sometimes when we like an object very much. One factor in this instinctual manifestation is again very evident, namely, the linking up of sexual pleasure with the anatomical and physiological conditions

---

[6] The term "phase" signifies the length of the abscissa, the term "level" the length of the ordinate, the term "organization" is used to signify the morphological and structural content of a graphically represented section of the libido development. These terms will however be used almost synonymously for the different sections of the development of the libido.

and its dependence on the instinct of self-preservation. The solid food given to the child at this time has to be prepared for digestion through biting and chewing. Biting at this early period, when the infant is quite unable to use any instrument, even his hands, is his first and only means of destruction—a very effective one because the chewing muscles, at this time, are the strongest in the body and the teeth the hardest organs.

During the period of the first sexual activity at the mouth zone, after the detachment of the pleasure-sucking instinct from the nutritional, the oral instinct finds sufficient satisfaction on the child's own body, but later, after the acquisition of teeth the instinctual activity demands an outside object. Pleasure-sucking is, after weaning, an auto-erotic activity; the child finds satisfaction on its own body and as far as the sexual instinctual satisfaction is concerned can almost do without the outside world and psychic relationships with it. However, with the beginnings of the pleasure in biting there appear very marked relationships to objects of the outside world. The connection between the pleasure-sucking infant of the biting phase and the objects which served his pleasure in biting, has to be regarded also as psychic. It is difficult for anyone who becomes acquainted for the first time with the analytical material of this period to imagine the extent of the pleasure-demand of the child at this time, and the psychic relationships resulting therefrom. However we can all recall the way older children play at biting and the pleasurable fear of being bitten or eaten up in animal games. At a later age in childhood we observe fantasies which are the expression of a psychic relationship to objects of the outside world, based on oral instincts. This psychic relationship to objects in the biting phase is also extended to the human objects, i.e. the persons in the child's immediate environment. These persons will, at least psychically, be brought into relationship with the oral zone, as are the objects on which the biting pleasure is experienced. In analysis, the psychic relationship to these persons will show characteristics which reveal clearly the pleasure in biting and devouring. I once analyzed an adult who, to a great extent, mentally, had not been able to get beyond the level of biting and chewing as pleasure gratification. If an object of the outside world, even a person, were to stimulate his pleasure, he would have an uncontrollable and of course unappeasable desire to put it into his mouth, to chew it and devour it, in other words, to incorporate the object orally. In his dreams, loved people would often appear in the form of tasty dishes. The earliest fantasies he remembered, from about the age of three, were of his mother being cut in pieces and cooked; these fantasies were accompanied by vivid pleasure feelings of an erotic nature. A great many examples of this sort can be found. Since children at this age cannot communicate their psychic experiences by language we have to draw conclusions about them through direct observation, or from the pathological relics of this stage in older children or in adults with whom, in analysis, we reconstruct the psychic experiences of the biting phase. Analysis of adults with abnormally strong instinctual relics from the biting phase, shows us the high degree of pleasure which can be attained through the actual or fantasied eating up of objects during this phase. Because of the instinctual tendency to devour objects, we consider we are justified in calling this phase cannibalistic.

Here we must mention a further characteristic of infantile sexual instincts. Almost every active sexual instinctual desire is associated with another of a similar nature, the aim of which is passive. An example of such complementary instinctual tendencies in the adult is the desire and activity of loving, side by side with the wish to be loved. In the child these antagonistic tendencies appearing simultaneously, though with opposing instinctual aims, are far more pronounced. Thus with the child and often with perverse adults who are unable to give up a phase of behavior belonging to early childhood, side by side with the wish to beat is the wish to be beaten; side by side with the wish to look the wish to be looked at, and also, in the biting phase, besides the wish to eat up exists the wish to be eaten up. It is difficult for normal grown-up persons to understand that being eaten up could represent the fulfillment of a sexual wish. However the analysis of certain neurotic persons shows this indubitably. We so often find that a child's neurotic fear of being eaten up by some animal or a giant arises from the defence against a profound desire for this passive pleasure satisfaction; in general, we find that every neurotic fear is the defence against a desire which has as its content that which is feared. This content is to be seen in many fairy tales, as for instance, "Little Red Riding Hood", "The Wolf and the Seven Kids". A famous fountain in Berne, Switzerland, which is called the "Kindlifresser" (Child-eater), shows a man devouring children. We find the same content in the Bible story of Jonah and the whale, and in the Greek myth of Cronos, the God of Time, who eats up his own children.

The fact that two instinctual excitations arising from the same fundamental source can be contradictory, one having an active, the other a passive instinctual aim with regard to the same object, justifies our use of the term ambivalence.[7] This ambivalence in the infantile instinctual impulses, if only dispositional, facilitates the reversal of an instinctual impulse into its opposite. Thus an instinctual desire with an active aim is frequently transformed into a passive one, if the desire is frustrated by the object's resistance and if the frustration is accompanied or followed by a painful experience. In this way, out of the wish to devour an object can arise the wish to be devoured. By means of psychoanalysis the original active, instinctual aim can be discovered hidden behind the passive one which is often more easily capable of becoming conscious.

The term ambivalence, which implies the simultaneous existence of two instinctual excitations of like content, such as, biting, looking, beating, copulating, but with contrary instinctual aims (active-passive), is mostly used in another sense, namely, for the divided attitude manifested in many single instinctual impulses towards an object. When the instinctual wish exists to devour an object, the attitude of the individual who wishes this is contradictory. In the attitude where the instinctual wish in the object relationship is to devour, the tendency to incorporate is manifested. This incorporation represents the most intimate

---

[7] This term, according to Ernst Bleuler, signifies "the same thing positively or negatively felt emotionally, or positively and negatively thought or striven for."

connection with the object which can be imagined, for the devoured object has an existence in the person who has devoured it, inasmuch as it can serve as nourishment and become part of the body through the assimilatory process of digestion. In this attitude, therefore, the desire to devour signifies the wish for the most intimate connection, the wish to have the object entirely for oneself. We may consider this instinctual tendency as positive or friendly. The second attitude towards the object, in the instinctual wish to devour, is negative or hostile, arising out of hate. The aim of this second attitude in the impulse to devour is to exterminate the object brutally, to destroy its very existence. We can hardly imagine a harder or more severe treatment of the object than its extermination through the act of eating.

In the, instinct to devour, therefore, the wish for the most intimate connection with the object comes to expression simultaneously with the wish to destroy its existence in the outside world, both instinctual tendencies being experienced as pleasurable. The fact that from a single instinctual impulse a positive attitude can arise simultaneously with a negative one towards the same object, has led us to call this instinctual impulse ambivalent. Ambivalence signifies that two attitudes in opposition to one another, one of which can be called friendly and the other hostile, can come to pleasurable expression simultaneously towards the same object. The most marked ambivalence, that is, where the two contradictory instinctual attitudes manifest the greatest difference and opposition, is the ambivalence of the second oral phase, the phase of the instinct for biting and devouring.

The term ambivalence is often used and characterizes very adequately certain forms of relationships between individuals. If one person is extremely dependent on another, but at the same time tortures him, we call this attitude towards the object ambivalent. Anyone can observe examples of such behavior in his own surroundings. Ambivalence is to be found throughout all the stages of infantile libido development but, with the progress of the development the intensity of the ambivalence, that is to say, the opposition of the instinctual tendencies—friendly and hostile—decreases. Only in the last phase of development, the final stage, which we call the genital level, does the ambivalence vanish to a great extent. If a relatively large amount of ambivalence continues until maturity, one can imagine how greatly the object relationships will be disturbed, for, simultaneously with friendly attitudes hostile, hatefilled attitudes and tendencies exist and try to manifest themselves towards the same object. The friendly attitude will be partially injured by the hostile one, the positive emotions will be partially able to suppress those filled with hate. This conflict however brings the danger of a neurotic disturbance of equilibrium in the psychic economy. Ambivalence, when still persistent in later periods of development, is an archaic heritage; with primitives, who are so much closer than civilized peoples to the earlier forms of the human species, ambivalence is very evident.

Within the period of the oral pleasure activity of the small child, we have now been able to differentiate between two levels or phases of oral pleasure activity in the infant; a primary or suckling phase—objectless and auto-erotic—and a secondary or biting phase, in which there is an object relationship of an ambivalent nature. The object relationship of the second oral level can also be designated as sadistic. By sadism we mean a pleasurable aggression against an object, aggression being the scientific expression for all actions of hostile and brutal intent carried out against an object.

If we wish to study carefully a specific instinctual satisfaction, particularly one originating at a primacy zone, we shall have to observe the vicissitudes of this impulse satisfaction during the subsequent development, beyond the time of the predominance of this particular zone. Here we shall have to anticipate the section dealing with instinctual vicissitudes and give a short general account of them.

Civilized man is able, even in later life, partially to hold fast to oral satisfaction. In the domains both of pleasure-sucking and of biting, much is granted him; he may smoke, may chew gum or tobacco, suck and bite candy, suck or chew pencils, and so on, in order to obtain oral satisfaction. Even in his adult sexual life, some satisfaction is still admitted. No one would care to give up the pleasure of kissing in a love relationship; we have mentioned the pleasure many people take in biting the object of their love; fellatio, or the performance of the sex act by the introduction of the penis into the mouth, is not infrequently practised, as is cunnilinctus, which signifies the approach of the mouth zone to the female genitals. Thus we find very many activities in the sexual life even of healthy individuals which have persisted from the phase of oral primacy, or from the oral organization, continuing even after sexual maturity.

In the neurotic rejection of the desire for pleasure-sucking, which leads to hysterical vomiting and loss of appetite, as has been described in the case of the little girl, a connecting link from the animal world often plays an important part. In these symptoms, there is a rejection of the male sexual organ resulting from the original attachment to the mother's breast, which is still present in the unconscious. The cow's udder, which a child usually has occasion to observe, often forms a bridge between the attraction and the rejection which leads to the conflict expressed by the neurotic symptom, for the cow's udder is situated where, in the male, the penis is found and the milk-giving function of the cow's udder is either demonstrated or explained very early to the child. Little five-year-old Hans, who was analyzed by Freud, cried out when he saw a cow being milked: "Oh, look! There's milk coming out of its widdler!"[8] This identification of the penis with the mother's breast is to be found in very many hysterical symptoms. The desire for fellatio is to some extent a displacement of the infantile desire for the mother's breast.

Oral instinctual energies and attitudes also find expression in the characters of certain persons. There is something persistently suctional about individuals with character trends belonging to the first oral phase; something extremely insistent, they attach themselves to their objects almost as if by suction and are very difficult to shake off. Others constantly relive the happy time of

---

[8] Sigmund Freud. *Collected Papers*. See Brill's *Basic Writings of Sigmund Freud*. Modern Library, New York.

carefree satisfaction at the mother's breast and with the substitute objects of the early oral period, showing a pathological, unreasoning optimism and unconcern regarding the cares of everyday life. Oral characters of the first level are generally very well satisfied and contented with themselves, but the people round them do not find them agreeable.

Sublimation of oral instinctual tendencies, that is to say, the deflection and utilization of these for cultural purposes, is essential for people who are ambitious to acquire knowledge and to make scientific investigations; the pleasurable assimilation of observed facts, as well as the findings and thought-processes of others can, for instance, in the case of scholars and scientists, be traced back to transformations of libidinal energies from oral sources.

If a person shows marked libidinal relics belonging to a phase which he should have outgrown and abandoned, we term this a fixation of the libido. Such a person experiencing a disappointment in a love relationship or in another libidinal satisfaction is likely to return to the phase of libido development at which he is fixated. A disappointment in a fixated person's love life, or in other satisfactions of his sexual instincts is likely to make him turn back to the instinctual satisfactions which he so much enjoyed at a specific period of libido development and which, unconsciously, he preserved in his memory. He then returns to the old satisfactions at this level or, in psychoanalytic terminology, he regresses to this level—the term regression signifying a movement in a backward direction on the course of a development which has already taken place. With all its strength, the conscious personality resists the recharging of past pleasure sources with energy, because the evaluation established by education, culture and society forbid these gratifications.

Thus a conflict arises between the Ego evaluations and the unconscious instincts craving satisfaction; this conflict finds expression in a neurotic symptom. Regression to the second phase of oral satisfaction is the basis for the severe psychic illness called melancholia. The latter is characterized by extreme depressions and low spirits combined with a distaste for life and bitter, unjustified self-reproaches. The patient mentioned above, who craved to devour every object he liked, whose fantasies were about his mother being prepared for oral incorporation by being cut up and cooked, suffered from depressions and low spirits so extreme as to approach melancholia.

The discovery of the mechanism of development of melancholia was made by Freud.[9] It was he who found out that the melancholic's terrible self-reproaches are in reality reproaches against a loved person in the outside world—the loved person having unconsciously been incorporated into the psyche by oral paths. The psychic devouring of the object is the consequence of a disappointment in the latter and signifies a regression to the biting, or cannibalistic, phase. Karl Abraham tells us of a female patient who, when suffering from a melancholic depression, constantly accused herself of having stolen.[10] Shortly before the outbreak of her illness her father had been put in prison for theft. This patient's self-reproaches were actually reproaches to her father or, in other words, to the introjected object, which she had incorporated into her own psychic personality. Psychoanalysis finds that introjection is a psychic incorporation through the oral zone, bringing about a friendly-hostile gratification, the nature of which is sadistic.

c. The First Anal Phase

In examining the first anal phase of the child's sexuality we shall be able, as before, to retrace the history of libidinal development. In this phase we come across instinctual satisfactions of an intense nature, originating at a region of the body which has an important function in self-preservation and which takes care of the elimination of the indigestible residue of food, namely, the lower intestinal canal, the anus and the surrounding region. From the standpoint of psychoanalysis the borderline between the oral and the anal region is the pylorus, at the sphincter of the stomach.

---

[9] S. Freud. *Mourning and Melancholia*. Collected Papers IV. Hogarth Press: London. 1934. p. 152.

[10] Karl Abraham. Selected Papers on Psychoanalysis. *Development of the Libido*. Hogarth Press. London. 1932. p. 454.

From the pylorus downward we find anal sexuality, from the pylorus upward we find oral libidinal tendencies. The eroto-genetic significance of the anal region of the body is particularly marked from the beginning of the third year till the end of the fourth, it is almost as important at this time as is the genital zone in adult sexuality.

The half liquid evacuations of the infant cause the first intense excitations of the anal zone; these excitations are the deter-minants in the subsequent intense desire for satisfaction. In discussing pleasure-sucking we said that for the child to desire satisfaction and to strive for the instinctual goal, he must already know what the specific gratification is, he must at least once have experienced the process which releases this satisfaction. The bowel movements and even more so the intestinal disturb-ances, constipation, flatulence, diarrhea, which neither sucklings nor older children escape, create, through a pleasurable stimulus, a model for the subsequent pleasure desire at the anal zone. The active interest in the child's intestinal processes shown by the nursing person serves to increase his interest in this region; we must remember too that his mind and faculties are developing already. We know what psychic significance is attached by many adults to the regularity or irregularity of their bowel movements and that such people transfer to the child their attitude towards their own anal functions. Many mothers are too ready to assist their children's sluggish bowel movements by means of an enema, which naturally gives an intense stimulus to this zone, a stimulus which is then connected with an object relationship. We have already mentioned the danger of a too abundant satisfaction at the oral region, this applies also to the anal zone. The instinctual drive at the anal zone can be greatly strengthened by accidental or outside factors, such as the behavior of the mother or nursing person.

How is the erotogenic sensibility of the anal zone utilized by the child? Children who satisfy themselves anally hold back their stools till the accumulation of these in the lower section of the intestine causes a violent contraction of the excretory muscu-lature. There is then a violent stimulus of the sphincter zone at the passage of the mass of excrement through the anus; intense sensual pleasure is experienced and at the same time a certain sensation of pain. Grown-up people, if they are honest enough to admit it, know and enjoy the sensual pleasure brought about by the passage of a large stool, of a stick-like form. The pleasure is however far more intense for the child at the anal phase and for older children and adults with anal fixations. Psychoanalytic experience shows that this pleasurable process of intestinal evacuation is a model of the subsequent genital libido processes and sensations. The content of the intestine is experienced in the same way as is subsequently the penis of the male, whilst the lower intestinal mucous membrane can be compared with the vagina. This pleasurable function of the evacuation of the intestine is, as will be shown, of great significance. In addition to the sexual pleasure procured through the lower intestinal canal and through the anal function itself, there are many other psychic manifestations connected with anal eroticism which it is difficult to represent systematically. These can best be understood by a discussion of their historical course. First of all, we must differentiate between the stages in the anal phase of the child's sexuality, in which two contradictory pleasure tendencies come separately to expression.

The first anal phase is distinguished by the predominance of pleasure experienced at the passage of the stool and its expulsion. Psychically, the expulsion of the stool signifies its destruction in a pleasurable-hostile intent. We know this from the analyses of adults, in whom a regression to this phase has occurred, in other words, where there has been a backward flowing movement of the libido, over the course of its former development, to the first anal phase. Love objects belonging to the outside world are at this phase identified with excrement. We shall see that this symbolic identification of love objects with excrement is, on the other hand, also the expression of particular esteem. In the act of expulsion however the hostile tendency of the instinctual satisfaction is predominant. The attitude towards the excrement as an expelled object is thus ambivalent; it is positive in regard to esteem and the wish to retain, and negative insofar as rejection and expulsion are concerned. People with fixations at this level react not infrequently to a disappointment in love, or of any other kind, with psychically conditioned diarrhea, signifying a hostile expulsion or rejection of the object. The desire for expulsion is a contributing factor in the cause of many neurotic symptoms, without forming the basis of any particular neurotic disease; however two kinds of psychotic diseases, melancholia and paranoia, are constantly preceded by a regression to this level, which leaves traces in the psychological trends of both these mental illnesses.

In order to understand psychosexual processes and object relationships a term must be explained which is constantly employed in psychoanalytic literature, that of object-cathexis. Cathexis signifies an accumulation of psychic energy in any one part of the psychic apparatus. Our sense organs receive innumerable perceptions and stimuli from every individual object in the outside world and these are experienced intensely if our interest in the object is intense. Intra-psychically, these perceptions form a unity of the ideas and memories which were experienced in connection with the stimulating object in the outside world. This intrapsychic unity of ideas and memories is termed the object representation. The psychic relations, changes of attitude, increase or decrease of interest, briefly, the processes of "cathexis with psychic energy," take place on the object representation. Some of these processes are expressed in the relationship with the real object in the outside world. A great many, however, remain in the interior of the psychic apparatus; even the varying intensity of interest resulting from the perceptions received from the object in the outside world is not immediately expressed in action towards the object; it is first expressed in feelings and thoughts, according to the increase or decrease in the cathexis of the object representation. An object relationship may never even be expressed to the object. A man may fall in love with an actress whom he has never seen off the screen or stage, the actress may be unaware of her admirer's existence, nevertheless he has effected an object relationship because the object representation of the actress, which is within his mind, has been cathected or charged with libido. It is easy to understand that countless psychic processes can occur in the idea and memory-unit we have of a person—which is called the object-representation—without a corresponding real action in the outside world; it is clear also that often there could be no such action, because interior and exterior inhibitions prevent the psychic process from being transformed into action towards the real object. The concept of object-representation will help us to understand the psychic devouring of an object either at the cannibalistic level, or in a regression to this phase, and how at the first level of the anal phase an object can be expelled psychically as excrement. These processes of psychic energy cathexis occur on the object-representation, independently of the real object or person, although they may be released by the behavior of the latter; few are transformed into real actions towards the object. Briefly, object-cathexis means a charging of the object-representation with psychic energy derived from the various instinctual sources.

d. The Second Anal Phase

We have observed that children who make use of the erotogenic sensibility of the anal zone, accumulate their stools in order to increase the pleasure of the passage and expulsion of the latter. In the second phase of the anal period of libido development, the chief pleasure is no longer experienced at the passage of the stool, but in holding it back. The accumulation of the stools, originally of indirect significance in anal pleasures, acquires, at this time, an independent pleasure-giving function. At this period of holding-back, of retention pleasure, as we call it, the stool, even when evacuated, is regarded as an enormously important and valuable object. The interest of the child in its stool is to a certain extent increased also by the behavior of the grown-up people. If one watches the obvious delight of the mother over her child's successfully accomplished bowel movement and her appreciation of the product, one may assume that this delight must awaken or strengthen an organically established libidinal interest on the part of the child.

The pleasure children take in their feces, which is to be observed very early, can seldom be expressed, because the educators prevent them from smearing objects and particularly themselves with feces. There are however adults who regress to the child-hood phase of taking pleasure in their feces. These are the psy-chotics, in whom a catastrophic loss of psychic inhibitions has taken place. Such people cannot be prevented as easily as chil-dren from pursuing their anal activity and they live out their pleasure in feces in the mental hospital, smearing themselves and everything within reach with their fecal matter. In child analyses, we often learn from older children of the relics of this early infantile pleasure in feces, of their toilet games, the carrying of excrement to secret places and so on.

The child's own evaluation of his stools and the joy with which the nursing person welcomes his bowel movements, strangely enough, makes him regard his feces as a demonstra-tion of his love and as a gift. The significance of the stool is extended to all the child's possessions, which is an important step towards the social adjustment of the anal tendencies and through which the child's possessions acquire value. The secret value to the collector of the objects he collects originates with the infantile evaluation of the feces. Furthermore, excrement passes on its significance to money. In the unconscious, gold and excrement and excrement and money are regarded as identical.

A few examples from various domains of human behavior will make clear the significance of excrement in regard to money and gold. The figure of the little personage expelling ducats, the "Dukatenscheisser", usually a small chocolate man in the act of expelling a gold piece from his anus, which used to hang on many Christmas trees in Austria, is the most striking example in this sphere. There is also the donkey from the fairy story "Table be Spread", from the front and back of whom gold comes out when the magic words are spoken. The thief's payment, of leaving his stool, before he escapes from the place where his deed was committed and the payment insolvent debtors were compelled to make in the middle ages, when they were put in the pillory after being given a drastic purge, leave little doubt that excrement and money are regarded as alike. People often talk of being "cleaned out" when they have no more money and of money itself as "chicken manure". A common expression for payday is "the day the eagle shits". In German speaking countries the merchant is also making use of the representation of money by excrement when he employs the same word for his day's "takings" as the hunter for the excrement of animals, namely, "Losung" or "droppings". The dreams of man are full of analogies between our most precious metal and its substitutes, and the most despised material we know, which once gave its significance and value to gold, money and possessions in general.

Education demands cleanliness, that is, restriction of the interest in excrement and punctuality of bowel movements. In other words, giving up the pleasure in retention and making other use of these instinctual desires. However, education does not always succeed completely in mastering these pleasure tendencies. As an extreme example, a patient, as a boy of 14, would postpone the evacuation of his rectum for hours until finally he would have to place paper between his underwear and his anal region, so that the stool spontaneously expelled through the violence of the stimulus, would not soil his clothes. Many people remain fixated at anal sources of pleasure and diverse neurotic manifestations can result from this fixation or from a regression to and revival of anal instinctual tendencies. In such fixated individuals there is often an undisguised revival of the gratification in holding back the stool, but owing to the Ego's rejection, the gratification is experienced emotionally as suffering. The result is often neurotic constipation, accompanied by a hypochondriacal interest in anal processes and in the stool itself, which must be considered as a return of the infantile interest in excrement and anal functions. However even with healthy adults, the interest in their stools does not entirely vanish, as is demonstrated in many of our jokes. A case of "touching phobia" will illustrate the extent of the neurotic's unconscious interest in excrement. We know from analysis that the fear of touching objects because they appear dirty or capable of spreading infection arises from the repressed desire for the anal erotic pleasure in touching the anal product. A man who suffered from touching phobia protected himself against direct contact with objects by means of toilet paper. Thus, through his protective action, he unconsciously treated everything as excrement, betraying the hidden source of his neurosis. From the defense measures one can imagine the prodigious quantity of interest in excrement which is effective behind such an obsessional action. A patient with a washing compulsion sat for as long as 36 hours in the bath tub in order to soak from her body the particles of excrement which she maintained still clung to her after a bowel movement. From these pathological manifestations of defense, we can draw conclusions as to the intensity of the instinctual anal energies of childhood and must therefore consider the urge of these instinctual components to be very great.

The child's anal sexual activity and the inhibitions formed by the educator during this phase are of far-reaching significance in the development of moral feelings. The child is called "naughty" or "bad" and scolded when he soils himself or holds back his stool and the first educational demands restricting the instinctual urges are related to the excremental and anal pleasures of the child. The fact that the first moral demands are of an anal nature has very much to do with the later and higher acquisitions of ethical and moral feelings of duty. The first guilt feeling is felt by the child after an anal breach of duty. This original guilt feeling is frequently found to play a part in the guilt feelings experienced later, which originate from the non-fulfillment of higher social and ethical demands.

e. Sadism and Masochism

With the beginning of the anal phase we observe in the child intense sadistic tendencies, that is, pleasurable aggression against an object. In describing the perversions we have already characterized sadism and its various forms of expression, ranging from the physical mistreatment of objects to psychic torture. The primary form taken by sadistic aggression during the anal phase is that of beating and for this the buttocks are the preferred zone. This region of the body is the periphery of the anal zone, which has been discussed as the most important source of libidinal excitations at this time. Thus there is an anatomical relation between anal and sadistic pleasure, which exists as much in the active pleasure of beating as in the passive form of pleasure in being beaten. We have used the term masochism for the passive instinctual aim of pleasure in pain, the chief example of which is the pleasure in being beaten. The erotogenic source of the sadistic tendencies is the striated musculature of the body. It seems significant that the goal of the preeminent sadistic action, that of beating, and the masochistic reverse side of this instinctual activity, is at the site of the most powerful musculature of the whole body, the gluteal region. In the original masochistic pleasure the skin of the body must be considered as the main erotogenic zone.

Beating however, as has already been mentioned, is only one example of anal-sadistic activity. In the description of oral instinctual activity biting was termed a sadistic action, that is to say, a pleasurable aggression against objects of the outside world. Other such aggressive actions are: scratching, pricking, cutting, burning, etc. An important sadistic pleasure source is the domination of the object and its subjections to the sadistic individual's will. On the other hand, obedience and humility bring masochistic pleasure. In civilized countries, the physical torture of human beings is not tolerated and efforts are made to prevent it with animals, this does not however stop wars, political party fights and sports such as boxing from being recognized and tolerated as heroic and honorable sadistic activities. Although unfortunately physical punishment is still considered a means of education by many people, education attempts to repress sadistic tendencies of a physical nature in the child; however they flourish all the more in the psychic relations of mankind and examples of this may be observed in every human relationship.

Within the anal organization we consider that there are two levels: the first is characterized by pleasure in the expulsion of the excrements. Insofar as this pleasure is connected with an object relationship, it signifies destruction of the object. Sadistic actions which belong to this phase have characteristic features.

They consist in trampling the object, smashing it to pieces, crushing it. Owing to a disappointment which he experienced during his analysis, the depressive patient whose fantasies were of his mother being cut up and cooked produced a fantasy concerning the analyst, in which the latter was ground up in a large meat-grinder and the mixture used for sausages. The oral nature of this fantasy is unmistakable: here something edible has again been made out of the object, but the sausage form, the crushing to pulp and the expulsion from the grinder belong to the first anal phase. In the first anal phase, that of pleasure in the expulsion of excrement, the sadistic tendency aims at the destruction of the object through brute force; this lies very close to oral destruction by mastication.

The sadistic impulses at the second anal level—that of pleasure in retention—are of a different nature. At this level, the aggression against the object does not lead to its destruction, the object is spared this brutal form of extermination. The most apparent characteristics of this second phase of anal sadism are a tormenting holding on to and mastery of the object, enclosing it, confining it and selfishly restricting its liberty. Here we find a parallel to the pleasure in the retention of the stool in the rectum. The connection between the pleasure in retention and sadism can be demonstrated by an example, not taken from the period of childhood, but from that of old age, when a partial regression to anal gratification is manifested after the loss of sexual potency. A well known comedy figure in the baroque and rococo period is the conceited old man suffering from constipation, who completely restricts his young wife or relative, as he does the content of his intestine, but is betrayed by the genital force of a younger rival and thus deprived of his anal sadistic satisfaction, at least in regard to the loved object. Rossini's "The Barber of Seville" is an example of this kind. The object relationship of the second anal phase is characterized by the inner bond with the object and the desire to cling to it. At this phase the term object-love can be used, since one of the outstanding tendencies in our love-relationships is the desire to cling to the object.

In their subsequent transformations the sexual instinctual

manifestations of the anal sadistic phase become of enormous importance in mental life; in pathological cases, they condition perversions, such as the insertion of the penis into the anus, which plays a great role in homosexuality; stimulation of the anus by the fingers, which is required by some people in order to have an orgasm, and other such practices are a direct continuation of anal-sadistic pleasure satisfaction. Slight indications of pleasure satisfaction at the anal-sadistic zone are also to be found in normal people, the buttocks being the preferred region for playful aggression at the preliminary stages and during the sexual act; another such indication is the preference for having relations *more ferarum or a tergo*. Slapping on the buttocks, a pleasure which many people can hardly deny themselves whenever they see someone stooped over, or sexual excitation at the sight of the rounded form of this part of the body, are all a direct continuation of the anal-sadistic phase.

Among the anal sublimations, that is to say, the deviations of the anal instinct towards aims which are sanctioned by culture, are painting and the plastic arts, which are the outstanding transformations of the infantile pleasure in excrement into creative activities in the domain of art. Generally speaking, every production of the creative mind, whether artistic or scientific is, to some extent, an anal production. Many of our most valued activities are, partially at least, psychological derivatives of our infantile instinctual urge to anal activity.

Healthy and pathological transformations of the instinctual energies from these early periods are of great importance. First of all we will examine the character traits resulting from anal sexual instincts. It has been seen over and over again that many people who, in their early childhood manifested exaggeratedly, over a prolonged period, all those forms of anal "naughtiness" with which children procure pleasure of the anal region, are later to be distinguished by three marked character trends: obstinacy, parsimoniousness and orderliness, the latter often amounting to pedantry. Psychoanalysis was thus justified in establishing a connection between the strong instinctual disposition and activity in childhood and the appearance of these character traits at a later time, and considers that anal and sadistic instinctual energies are absorbed and come to expression through these character traits. In orderliness, sadistic and anal elements are discharged, in parsimoniousness there are more anal elements, and in obstinacy sadistic elements prevail. In our everyday language the connection between miserliness and retention of the stool is expressed in the saying: "He's so tight he couldn't pass a raspberry seed".

The simultaneous appearance of these three attributes in a typical character formation—Freud speaks of the anal triad of character trends—demonstrates clearly the inner connection between anal and sadistic instinctual sources at the origin of these trends, that is, at the second anal level of libido development. The innumerable processes of organization and order which are essential to knowledge, science, industry, social activities, hygiene, cleanliness and many other valued attributes of mankind have their origin at the anal zone.

The second anal phase of the libido organization has great significance in the origin of obsessional neurosis. Obsessional neurosis originates in a defence against the tendency to revive anal-sadistic sources of pleasure. The man who had to use toilet paper to protect himself from the direct touch of any object and the girl with the washing obsession are cases of obsessional neurosis. We have already mentioned the anal elements in these neurotic manifestations. Sadistic tendencies also exist in the tremendous hostility and fanaticism for order which are to be seen in the compulsive neurotic; compulsive neurotics often develop an exaggerated kindness and pity as a defense against their sadism; on the other hand, they involve relatives and friends in their obsessions, they keep other people in a continual state of tension and suspense and are able to derive much sadistic pleasure from their complicated neurotic activities. In this connection, you will remember the case of the girl with the washing obsession, who insisted on sitting for 36 hours in the bath tub to soak off the particles of excrement she thought still adhered to her body, while her mother had to warm the water for her bath on the kitchen stove.

We have already mentioned that the anal activity of the small child at the age of two until four years is the model of the subsequent genital activity of maturity, the penis being represented by the fecal stick and the vagina by the rectum and anus with their mucous membranes. Since, at the anal phase, the two organs necessary to the pleasure process belong to the child's own body, no partner thus being necessary, we call these pleasure processes at the anal zone auto-erotic (autos=self. Gr.), which means processes in which the individual is sufficient to himself, requiring no object in the outside world for his satisfaction. However at a very early age the stool is identified with objects of the outside world and at the same time sadistic and masochistic desires are directed towards these objects. Thus the anal pleasure processes are linked up with numerous object-relationships. Sadism plays an important part in the later love relationships between the sexes and it is one of the sources of energy in the masculine pleasure in possessing the object; masochism is the forerunner to the female pleasure in being conquered and possessed.

Owing to the paradigmatic function of the anal processes parts of the anal function and its evaluation are frequently carried over to the genital level. In the case of neurotic anal fixations, this can seriously interfere with the functioning of the genital sexuality of the individual. A derogatory, anal evaluation of the vagina is made sometimes by alluding to it as an unclean region, comparable with a toilet or a sewer. This contempt for the female genitals which originates at the anal region can seriously interfere with the potency of the man; the psychic relationship with the female sex will be greatly impaired if this attitude is transferred to women in general and they are regarded merely as a means of discharge of the genital products. A man who has this kind of attitude will look upon the sexual act as something indecent and dirty and will finally become incapable of love or turn to homosexuality.

If certain qualities pertaining to the feces are transferred psychically to the penis, the daily loss of the feces will excite the unconscious fear that the penis too might be lost, thus greatly accentuating castration anxiety, of which we shall speak later.

The identification of the anus with the vagina helps to promote a feminine attitude in men who incline to passive masochistic behavior, both through their own constitutional tendencies and as a result of their individual childhood experiences. The identification of anus and vagina makes it possible for such men to have feminine experiences on an anal instinctual basis. Their own anus then has for them a feminine-pleasurable significance, the significance of a region which could be threatened by or be accessible to the penis of another man. Numerous enemas administered in early childhood can strengthen this feminine attitude on the part of the man. Masculine pride and the fear of being treated as a woman, that is, of becoming like a woman, without a penis, makes such men resist the masochistic feminine-anal attitude; a psychic conflict results from this which often ends in a neurosis. Of even greater significance is anal sexuality in the mature sexual life of a woman. Normally the vagina has to take over some of the pleasure qualities of the anal region, if the sexual gratification here is to be complete. In the unconscious sexual life of the woman, birth has often an anal significance and her unconscious evaluation of the feces is transferred to the child. Mothers with highly developed anal trends express them in an exaggerated interest in the anal processes of their children; thus, even if there is not a particularly marked anal disposition in the child his anal-erotic tendencies may be encouraged and they may become pathogenic.

The fantasies belonging to this period are conditioned by the sadistic-anal organization. We observe that all children are extremely interested in the sexual activity of adult persons and that they make every effort to gain information. These attempts are almost always prohibited by the adults because they are helpless to deal with them. The child unable to find out the truth invents theories about sexual activity and childbirth, in which at the anal period, the anus and rectum play the principle role. As an example, a four year old child thought that in their sexual relations the parents press their buttocks together and children of this age are usually convinced that new-born babies come out of the anus. This idea became a certainty to a little boy when he heard that new-born babies are bathed after birth. He thought that the excrement still adhering to the babies had to be washed off. We find an allusion to the anal theory of birth in the mythological conception of man being made by God out of dirt or clay.

From these fantasies we shall again be able to see why we are justified in speaking of the primacy of the anal zone. The entire psychic activity of the child at this time overflows with anal and sadistic impulses which dominate and determine his thoughts, conceptions and fantasies. At the same time, fantasies about beating and being beaten and other sadistic actions can be traced in all children at this phase.

The resemblance between the second anal organization and the next phase is that the feces and the intestinal mucous are used as stimulating and stimulated parts, as are subsequently the genitals. In the second anal phase there is also a closer relationship with the objects of the outside world, usually with the parents and the brothers and sisters; this is further developed in the subsequent genital phase.

f. THE GENITAL PHASE

Certain traits in the genital phase of infantile libido development, which healthily have to be overcome before maturity, made Freud decide that the genital phase of childhood could not be taken as a complete model of adult sexuality, but rather as a transitional, intermediate phase, level or organization. This will be clear when we learn that at this time, with both sexes, the Phallus, which is the Greek word for penis or male organ, plays the principal part as the executive organ of sexuality. How can this be true in the case of the female sex? The female too possesses a small organ somewhat similar to a penis, which lies above the urethral opening; it is enclosed by the upper margins of the labia, and its form and position correspond to those of the man's penis and, when greatly developed, it can appear just like a penis. This organ which is homologous to the penis is termed the clitoris. It is the zone of primacy, as is the male penis which it resembles and to which it is analogous, in the phallic phase. This phase is termed phallic, because with both sexes the primacy zone is the phallic organ. The excitation of the genital zone, in the case of the male at the penis, particularly at the glans, in that of the female at the clitoris and the surrounding labia, is brought about through a rubbing movement of the hand, also often with girls by a rhythmic pressing together of the thighs. The manual stimulation of the genital zone is termed masturbation or onanism. In general, the vagina has not at this stage been discovered by the female child, that is to say, the pleasure sensation of an oral and anal character which later characterize the erogeneity of the vagina have not yet been transferred to the latter. The stimulation which makes the child aware of the possibility of obtaining pleasure at this sexual zone is produced by secretions from this region, by the urine which, particularly with the little girl, comes in contact with the genitalia, by the secretions of mucous from the vagina, the secretions of the preputium and by the decomposition of these different glandular secretions after having remained for sometime in this region. All of these discharge-products lead to irritation and sensations of stimulation, the removal of which by scratching or rubbing leads to the discovery of the erogeneity of this zone, that is, to its possibility of producing sexually exciting stimuli. The physical care of this region, washing and other hygienic processes such as powdering, putting ointment on sore places, all draw the child's attention to the possibility of sexual excitations at this zone. Even the clothing of small children is so made that it rubs them between the legs, thereby stimulating this region. Toys, such as rocking horses, bicycles, even the way children ride on the foot or leg of an adult, all bring about the same kind of stimulation. Masturbation becomes the predominant satisfaction at this phase which lasts from approximately the fourth till the end of the fifth year.

The male penis is extraordinarily highly esteemed at this time by boys and girls. The little girl soon discovers the rudimentary form of her substitute for a penis, is inconsolable and attempts in many different ways psychically to overcome this defect, whereby the most diverse mental attitudes and neurotic symptoms can be formed. We all know the type of woman who, because she will not admit the lack of what she considers the most important organs, behaves, feels and often thinks as though she were a man; in this way developing a masculine type of character. The bewilderment and feelings of inferiority of many women is the manifestation of a profound shock dating back to the time of the first realization of this supposed organic deficiency. The high esteem in which the penis is held makes the little boy fear a possible loss of this organ; he then develops castration anxiety. This anxiety concerns the penis, not the testicles, and originates partly from the fact that the fecal stick which, at the anal phase, is regarded as similar to the penis and is highly valued, is always lost. Another "forerunner" or "model" of castration is the loss of the mother's breast in the process of weaning. In addition to these models of castration, real or imaginary threats are directed against the penis as a punishment for masturbation. The discovery that there are human beings without this important organ horrifies the little boy. He thinks that little girls once had a penis like his—he cannot conceive of a living being without such a thing—but that as a punishment for masturbation, they have lost it.[11] This is the reason for his great anxiety about his penis; it is manifested in the most diverse forms of neurosis and is only comprehensible if we realize the immense significance of this organ in connection with the sexual pleasure, even of the little boy. In the small boy's fantasies of this period and as the corresponding basis of subsequent neurotic symptoms, the idea that the woman possesses a penis like the man plays an important part and is often obstinately retained, because it gives protection against the thought of the possibility of the loss of his own penis. In the unconscious fantasies of the neurotic, the mother, possessed of a penis, plays an important part.

The female often compensates and attempts to drown the profound depression which comes through seeing that the male

---

[11] Freud describes how little five-year-old Hans considers his penis so important that he discriminates between living and lifeless objects according to whether they have a penis or not. See Brill's *Basic Writings of Sigmund Freud.* Modern Library, New York.

possesses more than she, by violent aggression and hostility against men in general. Through this attitude, homosexual tendencies are increased and various character peculiarities and eventually neurotic symptoms result.

In the genital Libido period there is one fact of far-reaching significance: the wishes and fantasies emerging from sexual excitation are usually directed towards one particular object, generally the parent of the opposite sex; thus the infantile genital organization is extremely significant for the sexuality of the adult, since the choice of an object of the opposite sex is now made. It is natural that this choice be made from the persons of the child's environment, from among those persons who, until now, have taken care of the child and satisfied his needs. All the sexual urges of the phallic phase, from the various erotogenic zones—are directed towards these persons. Usually the object of the instinctual aim is the parent of the opposite sex. The processes of excitation are naturally centered around the genitals with their strong erogeneity; the other instincts subordinate themselves more or less to the genitals, the individual erotogenic zones giving what we call "fore-pleasure" in the sexual activity of normal adults, and serving to increase the final pleasure. We term these subordinate instincts *partial impulses* as distinguished from the main genital impulse.

In this phase, the love object is valued not merely during the periods of satisfaction of the sexual urges—whether these actually occur or whether they only take place in fantasy—it is valued continuously and, owing to the development of tenderness and affection, a more stable and lasting relationship is achieved. It is inevitable that the parent of the same sex, in the case of the boy, the father, in the case of the girl, the mother, should have a disturbing influence on this erotic relationship and that, as rival and competitor, his or her absence or death should be desired. The aggressive tendencies of this period accumulate against the rival and lead to the wish that he might die, or since so much value is attached by the boy to his own penis, he wishes that the rival, the father, might be deprived of his penis, i.e. castrated.

This is the situation of the Oedipus Complex.[12] Disappointments in the parent of the opposite sex lead to hate-impulses against this parent which can revive earlier relationships to the parent of the same sex and thus give an opportunity for the permeation and super-imposing of impulses and object relationships, both friendly and hostile, which play such an important part in neurosis.

The progress from the phallic organization to the final phase of infantile genitality can be accomplished by the male child with relatively slight transformations. The only condition necessary is the anxiety-free recognition of the fact that a woman does not possess a penis. In the case of the female, this step towards complete genitality is accompanied by difficult reorganizations. The female has to forsake the phallic organization, she has to give up the pleasure-satisfaction obtained from the substitute penis—the clitoris—which is masculine and active in its tendencies, and transform the active-aggressive instincts into feminine-passive ones. This transformation is not completed during childhood, but during puberty and subsequently; it occurs partly through a return to past libido positions, that is to say, through partial regression. This pregenital libido revival does not normally take place at the old erotogenic zones. Although, as a result of the partial regression, the specific erogeneity is reawakened, these zones are given up in favor of the vagina. The vagina takes the penis as the mouth did the nipples of the breast at the oral stage, and is stimulated by the movements of the penis as was once the anal mucous membrane by the expulsion of the feces during the anal phase. Pregnancy too, which is a part of the healthy fulfilment of female sexuality, and birth, bring libido satisfaction both of an anal and masochistic nature. These dynamic additions of pregenital instinctual energies, which are of a regressive type, retain the woman at the pre-genital phases; the masculine instinctual satisfaction which she at least temporarily enjoyed as a child, holds her back at the manlike, phallic phase; this makes it extraordinarily difficult for

---

[12] In the Greek Tragedy, *King Oedipus* by Sophocles, Oedipus kills his father and marries his mother, without consciously knowing that they are his parents.

the woman to attain a normal sexual function with vaginal sensation and gratification. Very often women do not succeed in attaining this and many have to be satisfied with substitute satisfactions at the clitoris or of another kind.

We have repeatedly emphasized the fact that instincts appear in pairs of opposites. In the oral wishes, side by side with the strong wish to devour is the wish to be devoured, in the case of beating we also find the passive opposite and, at the genital level, we find masculine trends of erotogenic instinctual pleasure in the woman, while in the man we find feminine trends. This constant instinctual ambivalence manifested by sexual currents with opposite instinctual aims, leads us to assume that the simultaneous presence and dynamic expression of contrasting pairs of instincts is based on the general organic constitution of human beings. This is termed the constitutional bisexuality of man. Constitutional bisexuality is being increasingly confirmed in all the fields of biological investigation. It is manifested in the fact that in human instinctual sexuality, two trends are present throughout each phase of libido development, one male-active, one female-passive. Constitutionally, we are to some extent like snails which, in copulation, carry out both male and female functions. The presense of too strongly contrasting elements of the opposite sex in the instinctual life, feminine in the man, masculine in the woman, predisposes the individual to neurotic illnesses, the ultimate condition of which will be found in a marked bisexuality on an organic basis.

The organic basis of bisexuality leads us to investigate the connection between the different phases of development of the libido with the somatic development of the human organism. In this connection, we find that there is a remarkable temporal difference between the ontogenetic and phylogenetic organic formation and development of an erotogenic zone, and the libidinal significance and use of this. We find an organic precursor of oral sexuality at a very early stage in the development of the human fetus. We must mention here that every single living creature, in its physical development from the impregnated ovulum, has to pass fleetingly and in an abbreviated form through all of those stages which the species, in the course of its thousands of years of development has slowly traversed (fundamental biogenetic law). We know, for instance, that at a certain period the human embryo has gill-clefts like the fish, that later for a short time it has a tail like a monkey, which it soon loses. Thus we see that the development of the species is repeated, at least allusively, in the development of the individual. During the first days of intra-uterine development, the fetus shows a similarity to primitive living creatures consisting of a few cells, which are called gastrulas, and which only possess one opening in their bodies, through which the sexual products, in the form of single cells, leave the microscopically small bodies. This opening is called the primal mouth; it is simultaneously the opening for nutrition and for the sexuality of this primitive creature. The generative activity of the primal mouth, with these creatures which correspond to the gastrula stage of the human foetus, can be recognized as a biological model of the subsequent oral sexual activity of the suckling.

At a later stage, in which the fetus is more developed, towards the end of the first months of pregnancy, we find the intestines terminating in the cloaca, which is at the same time the opening for the urinary products. In animals, corresponding to this stage of development (the *Ornithorhyncus paradoxus*, or duck-billed platybus), we find that the cloaca serves for the evacuation of the intestines as well as for the discharge of sexual products. The cloaca and its function with primitive animals can be considered as the organic model of anal sexuality. The mental or instinctual manifestations of the erotogeneity of these two zones—the mouth and the anal zones, occur at a much later period in the development of man than the embryological manifestation. It is as though the individual, even in his instinctual life has to repeat, in his experiences and actions, the history of the bio-sexual development of the species; this is of course only possible after birth, when emotional experiences are able to take place through the development of consciousness and when object relationships are established.

The bisexuality of the genital phase corresponds to the hermaphroditism in the normal physical development. The relic of this in the female is, as has been described, the clitoris; in the male it is a small depression in the colliculus seminalis in the urethra: this depression is called "utriculus masculinus" (male uterus) and corresponds in development to the female uterus, that is, to a pronouncedly female organ. At a certain stage of intra-uterine development, in which the fetus already has much that is human in appearance, one cannot differentiate between the sexes without making a microscopic examination, so closely do they resemble each other. The organic similarity of the sexes during this stage of development is again subsequently experienced in the psychological bisexuality of the individual at the genital phase.

In order to achieve greater clarity in our description, the individual phases have been more sharply defined and the process of development from one phase to another has been represented more simply and schematically than occurs in reality. Actually the predominance of an erotogenic zone and the organizations dependent thereon are relative. Side by side with the activity of the predominant zone by which a phase is named, we also find manifestations belonging to the subsequent zone, as though in anticipation or in recollection of the course of development. In addition to the primacy zone, other erotogenic zones play an important part as sources of excitation in infantile sexuality. Among these, the eyes and their function of vision are particularly prominent. Looking at the naked body, particularly at the genitals or buttocks of others, produces, from a very early age, intense pleasure satisfaction. Even with adults, the sight of the loved object is frequently the first source of excitation. In the case of perversion, the erotogenic pleasure in looking leads to scoptophilia. Being looked at when naked also often excites intense, even ecstatic pleasure of an undoubtedly sensual nature in children. This pleasure is the exclusive satisfaction of the exhibitionist. The active pleasure in the movement of the whole body in swinging and rocking have already been described. Affective processes, that is to say, emotions of the most diverse kinds, have at times the effect of violent sexual excitement on the child.

With children, anxiety can awaken, apart from painful sensations, a peculiar, tense pleasure feeling. Anticipation leads to such excitations; fright, confusion over something unexpected or missed may become sources of sexual excitation. Concentration of the attention upon an intellectual accomplishment of any kind is at times connected with sexual pleasure feelings. Many school children thus experience sexual pleasure sensations, or at a corresponding maturity, real pollutions during school work or in examinations. Briefly, a variety of sexual excitations provide for the disquietude which is the fate of the human psyche from childhood upwards, owing to its fundamental instinctual basis. It is worth noting that the individual sources of excitation can replace each other and that the partial impulses can thus substitute each other. Failure to obtain satisfaction at one zone causes an increase of sexual activity at another, which gives us the impression that the libido, that is to say, the sexual instinctual energy, is displaceable as though it were a fluid in a system of communication.

In the development of the libido, the advance to the next phase and the relinquishment of past phases cannot be regarded as occurring continuously in a forward direction. Parts of the libido advance, parts remain behind, other currents turn back to earlier cathexes, although often in a changed form, so that actually there is only a general impression of a forward movement, or more exactly of an oscillation, with a noticeable tendency towards maturity. The individual phases of the movement in this oscillation are caused on the one hand by inner organic processes of development and on the other, by experiences in the outside world. The outside experiences may have either an inhibiting or a liberating effect; however, they can also, through opening up wider possibilities, retain the libido, or have the effect of a decoy inducing a return to previous gratifications. Thus, with children, the forbidden genital activity results frequently in constipation or in a return to finger-sucking, and watching the intestinal pleasure of a little brother or sister may recall the attention to the old anal pleasure; a severe interference with anal instinctual satisfaction may cause an increase of the genital

masturbation. Generally speaking, the progress of libido development is slow and, accordingly, we speak of the "viscosity" of
the libido.

g. The Latency Period and Puberty

At the conclusion of the fifth year, the first important period
of sexual development is ended. The growing individual enters
a period of calm in the domain of instinctual satisfaction. Masturbation usually ceases, playing with the excrement and other
forms of "naughtiness" decrease or are given up. There is usually
a more or less stable truce in the struggle of the object relationships within the oedipus complex, owing to the identification
with the parents. But in this latency period, which lasts until the
beginning of sexual maturity, sexuality has not disappeared, it is
merely latent, that is to say, it is present but hidden, making no
obvious manifestation. The instinctual energies of the sexual
impulses are used for adaptation and adjustment which have to
take place at this time and for intellectual expansion and increase
of knowledge; the latency period is the period of sublimation.
But we find, in spite of the apparent calm of many children that
there are either masturbatory activities or psychic manifestations
corresponding to the tendencies of the oedipus complex, or
regression to pregenital instinct motions. The neuroses of this
time, predominant among which is compulsive neurosis, also
prove the existence of different forms of sexual excitation in the
latency period.

Between the 12th and 14th year, great quantities of sexual
excitation emerge, which arise from organic sources, as is indi-
cated during the maturation of the sexual apparatus, particularly
in menstruation with girls and in nightly pollutions with boys.
This leads to a powerful revival of psychic sexuality which is
similar in its aims at this time to that of adult persons, although
the objects are still unconsciously those of infantile sexuality
and the incest barrier prohibits their attainment. A relatively
long time is required before the infantile relationships are broken
off and the libido is transferred to acceptable new love objects.
The ultimate sexual satisfaction is then attainable. As long as the

incestuous objects predominate in puberty, the sexual activity and gratification is masturbation, which in both male and female brings about intense pleasure sensations of an explosive character. With the girl, the seat of the pleasure sensations is still chiefly at the clitoris and usually not until there has been sexual intercourse is the new area of pleasure in the vagina revealed, with its marked oral and anal mechanisms of satisfaction. A picture of adult sexuality can be formed from the slightly perverse deviations which are permitted, and from the relics remaining over from former stages of development in all their manifold variety. In healthy individuals the genitals are always the main executive organs of sexuality and are the site of the greatest psycho-sexual pleasure. In the full pleasure-functioning of the genitals sexuality and propagation coincide and combine in the most intense pleasure experience.

The neurosis of the genital level is hysteria, a psychic illness which takes the most diverse forms. In hysteria different varieties of anxiety, the transformations of psychic contents into somatic symptoms such as paralysis, muscular attacks, pains, disturbances of the functions of the organs are all connected with emotional disturbances. Hysteria results from a repression of genital, or more correctly, of phallic impulses, since, in this neurosis the rudimentary phases of childhood have not entirely been surmounted, and therefore there is still a strong connection with incestuous love objects. Hysteria frequently makes use of regressions of the libido which are due to partial fixations and so we find a combination of anal and oral, but mostly oral traits in its manifestations. The clinical symptoms then appear to be pregenital and it is only through analysis that we are able to trace the quantities of genital instinctual impulses which are the energetic source of hysteria; the genital wish then finds its expression in apparently pre-genital symptoms. For instance, cases of hysterical vomiting are manifestations of the wish for fellatio, as is shown by the connecting link between the cow's udder, the nipples of the breast and the male sexual organ. The wish for fellatio is actually a vaginal wish, appearing under the mask of oral desires and their defense.

CHAPTER FOUR

NARCISSISM

So far we have described the auto-erotic processes, that is to say, the sexual processes which attain satisfaction on the individual's own body, and the sexual relationships to the objects of the outside world during the various phases of libido development; we still have to deal with one libidinal relationship which continues throughout all these periods. Not only objects of the outside world, not only one's own body, but also important parts of the psychic personality are charged with libidinal energy. There is an organization within the psyche, a permanent formation, to which belong the most important functions which connect us with the outside world and to which belongs the function of consciousness. We call this organization the Ego. The Ego also contains the memories of the bodily perceptions of the individual and his psychic experiences; it has to be considered as the intra-psychic representation of the individual's own personality. And here, as with other object representations, cathectic processes take place though in much greater quantities and varieties. The cathexis with libido from various organic sources of this representation of the self which we call the Ego, takes place very extensively at a time when the Ego first develops as an organization of memories and of conscious psychic experiences. This cathexis of the Ego with libido brings about the phenomenon which Freud has termed narcissism. The phenomenon of being in love with oneself supplies us with a useful paradigm for narcissistic processes. Extreme manifestations of narcissistic behavior consist for instance in caressing oneself as one would another love object, of having thoughts and fantasies exclusively about oneself. An adult female patient who was in analysis with me, showed narcissism to such a marked degree that she could develop no satisfactory relationships with anybody. Whenever she read in the newspapers of an accident, she would immediately think that the persons killed could not have thought of her at the moment of death and that now it would be impossible for them ever to think of her, that she could never now have the satisfaction of knowing that they had thought of her. This extraordinary and painful mental condition was even manifested if a disaster occurred in another part of the world, when it was of course quite impossible for any of the persons involved ever to have the slightest idea of the girl's existence. The self-love or self-importance, in other words the cathexis of the Ego with libido, was so accentuated in her case that she could hardly bear the pain of knowing that there were people in the world who would never even think about her. Such thoughts show what importance and significance the self can acquire through extreme narcissism. With marked pathological cathexis the Ego, which, even in the normal individual, is experienced as the centre of his world, attains pyramidal proportions in comparison with which other people have merely the significance of grains of sand in the surrounding desert.

The turning of the libido towards the Ego, that is to say the cathexis of the intra-psychic representation of the individual's own personality with instinctual energy, is a necessity and is only abnormal when the quantity of cathexis is either too great or too little. Through narcissism, the instinct of self-preservation obtains powerful additions of libidinal energy, which strengthens the individual in his struggle for existence. The narcissistic cathexis of the Ego is extraordinarily high with the small child, greater than in the case of the girl who wanted to be in the thoughts of the whole of mankind. From the behavior of the primitives who have remained at abandoned phases of the development of cultural mankind and from the behavior of neurotic persons who have remained fixated at an earlier level, we are able to estimate the power and magnitude of self-love. Thus the child who has the same self-love and self-esteem as the primitive cannot do other than regard his thoughts and wishes as omnipotent. The magic actions of the savages and of the obsessional neurotic, who regard a thought or a wish as identical with a deed or an outside happening, are consequently a result of this feeling of omnipotence and cannot be considered as meaningless superstition if they are understood as caused by hypertrophic self-love. This omnipotence of thought is a result of narcissism and derives from libidinal sources. The savage by piercing the heart of an image of his enemy, thinks that he has killed him and believes firmly in the effectivity of such witchcraft; this attitude is only comprehensible if we realize that it is an expression of extreme overestimation of the wishes and thoughts, which are considered as immediately effective in the real world.

We can understand that the representation of the individual personality, that is the Ego, is the most important and most elaborated representation, since it contains many more sensations and memories than can be brought by any object. Object representations which appear later, are to a great extent formed according to the child's Ego; he learns only gradually and with difficulty that other objects differ from his Ego. In the case of markedly narcissistic persons, the object representations of other people remain similar to the individual Ego, and are usually only charged with sexual energy because they are similar to the self. As an example, the narcissistic male homosexual only charges with energy objects which are similar to his own sexual formation. Other object cathexes are narcissistic insofar as the object is as the individual would himself like to be, he then loves his ideal in the object, or he loves it because he once resembled it, as in the case of love for one's own children. There are, however, also object cathexes in which the object has been chosen from the standpoint of its utility or for its ability to satisfy the needs of the Ego.

We find that the marked cathexis of an object with libido brings about a decrease of the cathexis in the Ego, which leads us to conclude that there is only a certain quantity of libido at our disposition. A great increase of object libido has the effect of decreasing the self-love and vice versa. Anyone loving very intensely will neglect his self-interest, because he will not have an adequate supply of libido for his own narcissistic cathexes; anyone loving himself greatly will therefore not be able to love anyone else intensely. Thus we see that self-love or narcissism and object-love are in opposition to each other; a part of this antagonism between the Ego, or the instinct of self-preservation, and the sexual instinct can therefore be understood as antagonism between self-love and object-love.

In the case of a violent disappointment in an object, the Ego can avoid the experience of pain which accompanies the reaction to the object-love by making itself similar to the object representation of this object, by "taking on the characteristic features of the object"; the Ego can then absorb the instinctual cathexes originally belonging to the object representation. This process is termed "identification"; the Ego after a disappointment in or loss of an object, makes itself similar to the object, identifies itself with the object. This identification has a libidinal origin of a narcissistic character and transforms object-love into self-love.[13] Identification, in the case of loss or disappointment forms a protection against suffering. An example will perhaps make this clear. An adult patient who wished to have analytic treatment because of his strong homosexual impulses and wishes towards boys of about twelve years of age, had been brought up by a governess who, during his childhood, had lavished upon him the most ardent love. This governess—he called her aunt—whose entire object libido was bestowed upon the child, came to live in his home soon after the mother's death. The aunt died when he was twelve years old. Apart from a single violent attack of misery during her last agony the boy showed no reaction of pain or sorrow, although hitherto his behavior towards her clearly showed the greatest affection and love. As he grew older and reached sexual maturity, it became clear that he could only give his libidinal interest to boys of about twelve years old, which he had ample occasion to do in his profession as a social worker. His love manifested itself in motherly care and pampering whilst, at the same time, he was a little severe in his insistence that his advice should be carried out, just as the aunt had been with him as a little boy. He had identified himself with her and actually

---

[13] Identification is not however always the result of an object loss or disappointment, it may also occur as the expression of love and esteem of an object.

loved himself in the twelve year old boys; he was thus able, through the unconscious identification with the aunt, to give himself his aunt's love in the identification with the boys of twelve. Not until he was undergoing analysis did he fall into a severe depressive phase, which was a delayed reaction to the loss of the aunt, from which he had previously protected himself, through the establishment of the identification. This example clearly shows the libidinal and defensive significance of identification after an object loss.

The narcissistic cathexis of the Ego with libido is, under certain circumstances, very apparent. We are obliged daily, to a great extent, to lay aside our object cathexes for six or seven hours, to suspend our interest in the outside world and to concentrate our libido on ourselves. We do this when we sleep at night. The contents of our dreams are modelled entirely according to our own desires and show our intense egotism and self-interest during sleep. They demonstrate more plainly perhaps than anything else the intense self-love which revives each night during sleep. I purposely say revive, because this condition of self-love was the original condition before any object relationships were formed. Self-love begins at an earlier stage of development and, with the exception of times when the individual is violently in love, is usually stronger, more persistent, than any other object relationship, as is shown by our dreams during sleep. Self-love is, according to Freud, the great reservoir of libido from which the object cathexes are drawn, and painful experiences with the object make the cathexis of the object representation recoil to the Ego as though a kind of elastic band connected it permanently with the Ego. An injury to the functions of self-preservation, or bodily harm, may lead to an immediate, if temporary withdrawal of outside object cathexis. An aching tooth can seriously affect a love relationship.

There are mental diseases which come about through a regression to the original, exclusively narcissistic neuroses, among which we include schizophrenia and paranoia. The lack of relationships, that is, the lack of object cathexes in schizophrenia, and the megalomania in both illnesses indicate, even in the manifest picture, the tremendous cathexes of the Ego with libido in these diseases.

The difference between auto-eroticism and narcissism still remains to be explained. Auto-eroticism signifies sexual excitation and removal of the condition of sexual stimulation at the instinctual source, that is, satisfaction of the sexual needs by the individual himself on his own body, without an outside object. Masturbation, which needs no outside object for its accomplishment, is an auto-erotic action. We know very well, however, that even with onanistic action the psychosexual stimulus is often afforded by an outside object. The term auto-eroticism only signifies the physical part in the process of satisfaction. The psychological basis of an auto-erotic action can either be object-libidinal or narcissistic. The patient mentioned, who could only love boys of twelve years, was often stimulated to masturbation when he caressed his own body and particularly the nipples of his breast. Here the form of masturbation was narcissistic; with others there is narcissistic excitement at the sight of the body in a mirror. The term narcissism signifies the cathexis of the representation of the self with libido. It is a mental condition, although the libidinal energy used for its establishment and maintenance originates from somatic sources of excitation. Auto-eroticism takes place at the source of libidinal excitation independently of the psychological situation. Auto-erotic actions can be the result of the narcissistic as well as object libidinal sexual tension in the mental apparatus. Auto-erotic actions occur before the psychic development has progressed so far as the stage where ideas and memories have been formed either of the individual's own self or of an outside object, in other words, before narcissism and object-libido are established. Auto-eroticism signifies therefore the physical discharge of sexual energies through adequate satisfaction at the instinctual sources, without the assistance of an outside object.

CHAPTER FIVE

THE VICISSITUDES OF THE INSTINCTS

Psychoanalysis recognized that the instincts are not merely organic sources of excitation, the removal of which is the main task of the mental apparatus. They must also be regarded as the motivating factors of our whole mental life, effective under many forms as sources of energy for the most diverse psychic manifestations, provided direct satisfaction does not render them inoperative. The various transformations which the instinctual processes undergo when there is no direct satisfaction are termed by Freud the vicissitudes of the instinct. The general task of the psyche is to control stimuli. The psyche attempts by suitable means to dispose of the specific excitation or, in other words, to discharge the quantity of energy which the stimulus has brought into the apparatus. From our presentation it will be clear that psychoanalysis has a dynamic conception of mental functioning. Freud found that in the domain of the psyche, as in the physical world, the processes become more comprehensible if we understand the forces which cause them or lead them to their manifestation. The frequent use we have made of terms taken from the dynamics of physics to describe psychic processes will have accustomed the reader to this conception. Terms such as *psychic energy, interplay of forces, cathexis, discharge of energy, accumulation of energy,* are used to designate quantities of energy and aid us to understand mental processes in psychoanalysis. The fundamental principle of physics, the law of conservation of forces, has also to be applied to psychic energy. Psychoanalysis cannot give a final definition as to what this energy is; the term *energy* is used as a working hypothesis, as in physics. It is, however, more than a working hypothesis, because the concept of force and effect is well known to everyone through their own psychic experiences. The concept of psychic energy is indispensable in making clear the various psychic manifestations and the processes underlying them.

The stimuli reaching the psyche release first of all intra-psychic reactions, chiefly of an emotional character, they then lead to somatic manifestations; we assume that these psychic and somatic phenomena, in the form of affects and actions released by a stimulus, cause a discharge of the energy which was introduced by the stimulus—somewhat as in the case of the reflex; in this discharge of the stimulus however the mental reflex arc is not always immediately recognizable, owing to the complicated formation of the psychic apparatus and the various transforming influences of past and present psychic experiences. Occasionally a stimulus operates as "release", inasmuch as it causes the discharge of far greater quantities of energy than it has introduced. However, the "reflex remains the model of every psychic activity".[14] When a sexual stimulus reaches the psyche, it is followed by a discharge or unloading of this energy in the various sexual activities, such as thumb-sucking, anal processes of one kind or another, or a genital action. Besides the physical satisfaction at the erotogenic zones, we have also to consider the psychic reaction to sexual stimuli, such as affects and emotions, as means of discharge of libidinal energy. An affect is a very composite phenomenon consisting of specific muscular and glandular innervations and the perceptions of these innervations, together with feelings of pleasure and pain. The production of such affects (sadness, joy, pain, disgust, shame and so on) signifies a discharge of the particular psychic stimulus which has caused the affect, that is to say, the psychic energy which has been brought in by the stimulus causing the affect is eliminated.

The regulation of the processes in the psychic apparatus and therefore the regulation of the actions and affect processes proceeding from or appearing in the psyche, takes place in accordance with a fundamental psychic tendency; this is the psyche's desire to be at peace or to regain peace. Expressed in the terminology of mental dynamics this means that the psychic apparatus will not tolerate any lasting accumulation of energy within

---

[14] Sigmund Freud. *Gesammelte Schriften*, II. Die Traumdeutung. Internationaler Psychoanalytischer Verlag, Vienna, 1925. p. 458. See Brill's *Basic Writings of Sigmund Freud*. Modern Library, New York.

itself; an increase in energy is perceived by the Ego as pain or "unpleasure", whereas the discharge or removal of accumulated energy is felt as pleasure.

The release of accumulated sexual energy in the adult sexual act affords the greatest amount of pleasure that can be experienced. But the discharge through affect-processes also has a pleasurable effect, as we see by manifestations of joyful excitation, by the release brought about by a storm of tears after grief, or the relief of an outburst of anger. The term pleasure-principle, or pleasure-pain-principle has been given to the regulatory mechanism by which the mental apparatus tries to avoid increase of tension and pain, and to get rid of unavoidable accumulations of energy as quickly as possible, thus gaining pleasure. This principle may be applied to almost all psychic manifestations since these are to be considered as discharges following an accumulation of psychic energy and are regulated by pleasure and pain.

A modification takes place in the pleasure-principle as the psyche matures. The small child learns that many kinds of pleasurable energy discharges are followed by an increase of energy in the form of the stimulus of painful consequences. He will therefore renounce certain satisfactions, such as thumb-sucking, or retaining his stool, or of having a bowel movement at a time and place of which the educator disapproves, because he has constantly had the experience that these satisfactions are followed by pain in the form of punishment or a withdrawal of love. The child recalls the pain of punishment and when he feels the stimulus to forbidden satisfaction he reacts with fear, which prevents him from seeking the satisfaction. On the other hand, the anticipation of an instinctual gratification may induce the child to endure pain for the sake of the subsequent pleasure, for instance, children are rewarded for undergoing disagreeable experiences, such as going to the dentist or doctor. Experiences therefore modify the original pleasure-principle, in that reality is taken into consideration. This means a decrease of direct and immediate satisfaction, but avoidance of subsequent pain. This modification of the pleasure-principle is termed the reality-principle. The site of the reality-principle is the Ego. The aim of education is to establish and elaborate the reality-principle within the psychic apparatus.

What happens when instincts and their quantities of energy fail to be discharged through satisfaction? This may be due to outside reactions, such as lack of a suitable object, or to inner reasons, such as that the consequence of instinctual gratification might be even greater pain than that of constant instinctual tension.

An indirect way of decreasing instinctual tension may be found. The adaptibility, the plasticity of the sexual instincts make possible a modified discharge. A permitted object may be substituted for a forbidden one. Instead of an unattainable instinctual aim, or one that is forbidden, one that is attainable is chosen, in fact the instinctual aim can be changed into its opposite; Freud has termed these various substitutes for instinctual satisfactions instinctual vicissitudes and he differentiates between four such vicissitudes. The unattainable instinctual aim can be transformed into its opposite, if this inverted satisfaction can be attained without the harmful effect which direct satisfaction would have brought; this naturally only applies to instincts which require an object for their satisfaction and which appear as one of a pair of opposites. We term this process reversal into the opposite. A simple example will demonstrate this process. It is very much easier for a child to achieve his desire to be beaten than to satisfy his desire to beat somebody; he has only to be troublesome and naughty in order to attain his goal. Usually the active instinctual aim is converted into a passive one. But the opposite may also occur if, for instance, a little girl has been bitterly disappointed in her passive love towards the father and then, or later tries with more or less success to dominate men, to act as a man herself, to force men into the passive role. The reversal of the instinctual goal becomes possible, as in this example, through an identification with the object of the unsatisfiable desire. The masochist is able, for instance, to enjoy the pleasure of beating through identification with the beater; through this identification he becomes to a certain extent the beater and indirectly enjoys the active pleasure of beating.

Usually the second possible vicissitude of an instinct—that of being turned back and directed against the self—can hardly be separated from the first. For instance, if a sadistic wish directed towards an object cannot be satisfied it may be directed against the individual's self and result in masochism. We recognize that the withdrawal of a libidinal tendency from the object representation and its establishment in the Ego must increase the narcissistic cathexis and that the object libido, as in the case of identification, is transformed into narcissistic libido. To attain the instinctual aim, which has now become passive, a new active object is sought out, the pleasure of which is enjoyed through identification. The scoptophylic instinct, like sadism, can be directed against the self, the aim is at the same time reversed from the active—to look (scoptophylia), to the passive—to be looked at (exhibitionism).

The transformation of the instinctual aim into its opposite and its direction against the self are roundabout ways of discharging energy. These paths of discharge are taken because the psyche wishes at all costs to have its tension removed in accordance with the pleasure-principle; in other words, the mind strives to discharge its accumulated energy. If a direct discharge has to be prevented on account of the reality-principle, that is to say, because pain may be anticipated as a consequence of the discharge, the psyche will seek a discharge by indirect ways. These indirect ways are what we have called the instinctual vicissitudes, the third of which is termed sublimation.

Sublimation is the process by which an instinct abandons its original aim, because, in accordance with the reality-principle, the aim if achieved will cause pain and has therefore to be avoided. The instinct then selects a new aim, which is permitted by the reality-principle and by the Ego because it is socially acceptable and of higher value. This displacement of the instinctual aim, which occurs in sublimation, indicates the characteristic plasticity of the sexual instinct and is the result of the looseness of the ties between the sexual instinct and the object. When a child gives up playing with feces and instead plays with plasticine creatively, this is a simple example of sublimation. The pleasurable playing with feces, once it was forbidden, brought pain; with the plasticine, the child continues his instinctual activity, he has chosen a substance of similar quality, of which the educator in no way disapproves.

In sublimation the aim can be displaced at varying distances from the original instinctual aim. The substitute may still show some of the qualities of the original pleasure object, as in the example of plasticine modelling, or there can be subtler, more indirect ways of attaining satisfaction. When, for instance, we interpret the scientist's activity as a sublimation of the child's sexual desire for knowledge, the connection with the original instinctual satisfaction is very indirect and distant. The greater the deviation from the original instinctual aim, the less intense the pleasure from the instinctual satisfaction, because the degree of the pleasure sensation depends on the amount of decrease in tension and the speed at which this takes place. The remotest deviations of the sexual instinctual aims are those where the instinctual energies are so completely desexualized that their connection with the original aim is no longer recognizable. We assume that in the psychic apparatus there is a constant reserve of desexualized energy at the disposal of the Ego which can be used to increase cathexes of various kinds. The process of thinking also takes place by means of displacement of small quantities of libidinal energy, completely removed from their original goal and must therefore be regarded as a libidinal process. The pregenital tendencies of childhood and the genital forces of puberty and adolescence are the most easily sublimated; the genital tendencies of the adult are more rigid in their instinctual aim and can therefore be sublimated only in small quantities.

The importance of the processes of sublimation for the various purposes of culture, social adjustment, human cooperation, work and self-preservation of the individual can hardly be overestimated. Without this capacity for sublimation we, as human beings, could not have achieved the distinction between ourselves and animals, of which we are so proud. We owe our culture to the plasticity of the sexual instinct, which is manifested in its vicissitudes.

A fourth instinctual vicissitude is repression. This is one of the most frequent vicissitudes and its failure is of paramount significance in the origin of neurosis. In repression the psychic cathexis is withdrawn from the idea which represents the instinctual tendency in consciousness. In this way, the representative idea is obliterated in consciousness; it becomes unconscious. The quantity of energy and the amount of affect attached to this idea are thereby completely removed. We may assume that the quantity of energy thus removed and completely detached from the idea, contributes to the creation and increase of the unspecified desexualized energy, which the Ego can then use for its various cathexes. Frequently the repression of an instinctual tendency is not entirely successful, it is only with difficulty and much expenditure of energy that it is kept from consciousness since the quantities of energy belonging to the instinctual tendency are constantly thrusting themselves forward towards the Ego's paths of discharge. Psychic counterforces, which we term countercathexes, are then needed to hold the idea away from consciousness and to force back the driving energy from the paths of discharge. The quantities of incompletely repressed affects are displaced frequently along the paths of associations of thoughts or feelings, until they attach themselves to ideas capable of becoming conscious in order to achieve indirect discharge. If the censoring Ego becomes aware of this, the newly cathected idea has to be prevented from reaching discharge and is therefore also repressed. If a repressed impulse should force its discharge in spite of the opposition of the Ego, it is only able to succeed in doing so in a relatively distorted form. This breaking through of impulses will be experienced by consciousness as painful. The resulting instinctual satisfaction which is experienced as pain, because the conscious personality opposes it, is the neurotic symptom.

That part of the psyche in which the instinctual tendencies must be regarded as constantly held under repression is called the unconscious or the Id. The existence of incompletely repressed tendencies creates constant efforts and expenditure of energy for the psyche and contributes greatly to the psychic unrest which is characteristic of mankind. In order to understand the mechanism of repression we shall have to explain the relation of anxiety to the libido. In his first papers, Freud observed that there was a striking relationship between anxiety and libido. He ascertained that certain sexual and particularly genital practices and behavior have a harmful effect if they interrupt or retard the genital libido process, thus preventing the genital libido energies from being discharged. The harmful effect is manifested in the form of anxiety, particularly in the case of interrupted coitus, when the final orgastic reaction is prevented or disturbed, or when intense sexual excitation is left unsatisfied. This discovery was of great therapeutic importance, for with the cessation of the harmful practice the anxiety disappears. Freud assumed that the relationship he had observed between anxiety and libido is causal and that the undischarged libido was transformed into anxiety. Clinical experience seems to justify the assumption that in certain circumstances libido can be transformed into anxiety. Later, however, Freud found that in order to understand certain psychic manifestations it must be assumed that there is a second connection between libido and anxiety, this time not directly causal. There is a form of hysteria in which anxiety is the most prominent symptom, it is therefore called anxiety hysteria (phobia). In anxiety hysteria the fear of loved objects or the fear of forbidden desires for these objects is displaced to animals, places and inanimate objects. One has to assume that in these cases anxiety is not caused by libido but is the result of libido, that the Ego fears the dangerous libidinal tendency and that the anxiety, owing to the intense sensation of pain which it creates is usually able to block libido processes. Libido energies demand discharge by means of emotions and actions. Only the Ego has access to those parts of the mental apparatus which creates emotions and actions, that is, to affectivity and motility. The Ego, on the other hand, has the function of connecting the self with the outside world, with reality; it is the site of consciousness. The Ego regulates the discharge of the instincts according to the reality-principle, that is in accordance with memories of past experiences which are stored up in the Ego. Many libido processes cannot be admitted by the maturing Ego, because they do not concur with the reality-principle. Even the small child is forbidden to chew and devour objects, to urinate or to have stools at his own free will, or to satisfy his genital or exhibitionistic desires with the parents, because our educational measures are such that the painful consequences following those instinctual gratifications prevent him from indulging in them.

By what means does the Ego prevent undesirable processes from taking place? The Ego gives a signal which acts as a warning when a dangerous instinct emerges. This warning signal is so painful that it results in the immediate repression of the dangerous instinct. The painful signal is anxiety. Repression takes place in the form of an accumulation of energy in the Ego which is used as countercathexis against the libidinal demands which arise from the urge of the sexual instinct. Anxiety, even though sometimes resulting from a hindered libido process is nevertheless the most effective means of preventing a libido process from occurring. Since most of the libido processes do not succeed in reaching their ultimate goal of adequate satisfaction owing to the opposition of the Ego, and since the number of repressed tendencies is so great in comparison with those which are tolerated, the conscious processes of the Ego have, somewhat exaggeratedly, been likened to an island in comparison with the ocean of the unconscious or Id, which is the site of the repressed tendencies. The repressed instinctual tendencies attempt constantly, according to the amount of energy they possess, to influence and modify other reactions permitted by the Ego, in order to obtain their discharge. Currents of energy are continuously passing from the unconscious to consciousness, they drive us, in addition to our dreams and errors, to the actions of varying importance which we accomplish without becoming aware of the forbidden satisfaction hidden behind the manifest motives. A great many of the libido processes which are not tolerated are discharged in a moderated form through the sublimations; the transformations of the instinctual goal into its opposite and its direction against the self operate as indirect discharges. The completely successful discharge of all genital energies in the sexual act signifies a tremendous release to the mental apparatus and prevents the regression to pre-genital instinctual forces.

Anxiety is therefore usually a danger signal sent out by the Ego in accordance with the all-powerful pleasure-pain-principle, in order to check libido processes and accomplish their repression.

CHAPTER SIX

REPETITION COMPULSION AND DEATH INSTINCT

When we investigate psychic manifestations, particularly the actions of mankind, we find conscious motives which are real and others which are merely apparent, which we call rationalizations. In the background of these rationalizations analysis finds instinctual tendencies of a forbidden nature, which are the motivating forces in these actions. Some mental manifestations however do not seem to follow the regulation of the pleasure-pain-princple in the psyche. Repetitions of undoubtedly painful actions or experiences are sometimes brought on by the person himself and for these the most careful analysis can find no adequate pleasure motive. A person finds himself over and over again in the same painful situation, for example in a torturing dependence on an unsatisfying love-object, in which the masochistic pleasure gain does not suffice as a motive. Analysis shows that the establishment of this painful situation is the repetition of one of a similar kind experienced during childhood. Freud considered that such repetitions oblige us to attribute to the psychic apparatus a general tendency to repeat what has hitherto been experienced. He terms this tendency the repetition compulsion. In its organic fundamental basis the repetition compulsion has been less explored than the sexual instinct. The passage through the various stages of the organic development of the human species during the process of the individual development of the human being (biogenetic law) may represent an organic parallel to the repetition compulsion in the mental field. The concept of the repetition compulsion is connected with the theory of instinct only insofar as, according to Freud, at the basis of every instinct lies the urge to regain an earlier tension-free condition.

This concept of the drive for the re-establishment of former conditions applies also to the instinct of aggression, that is, of hostile and violent action against objects of the outside world, which, in sadism, is combined with libido and experienced as sensual pleasure. According to Freud, the fact that every human being is doomed eventually to die, or in other words, to experience complete destruction, has a causal connection with the aggression which every human being manifests towards outside objects. Freud formulated the hypothesis that in every human being there is a tendency to self-destruction, an instinctual urge towards death, which, in the last analysis, is the consequence of the all powerful longing for a completely tension-free condition. Freud calls this tendency the death instinct. The aim of the death instinct is to regain an earlier condition, since all that is living originates in the anorganic, the lifeless. Every individual cell in the organism is the site of this non-erotogenic instinct whose urge to self-destruction sooner or later is fulfilled. The life-preserving libido, the aim of which is always to gain pleasure, binds these destructive tendencies of the death instinct, unites them to the living organism and thus deflects the dangerous urge of this death tendency to the outside world. Through their connection with the Eros, aggressions directed towards the outside world have the effect of relaxing tension and are experienced as pleasurable; this erotic aggression is termed sadism. Sadism frees us thus from the tendency to self-destruction and the urge to self-preservation makes it comprehensible that human beings often harm and destroy objects on a much larger scale than is consistent with their struggle for existence. The turning of the death instinct against the self in masochism, and its accumulation in the institution of conscience and in the form of guilt feelings, are examples of the manifold transformations and changes undergone by the psychic processes, owing to the power of the death instinct and the exertions of the Eros in order to postpone the final fulfillment of the inner need to die. An exact representation of Freud's theory of the death instinct, which is still a subject of controversy, lies outside the limits of an introduction to the theory of the libido.

It has been the writer's intention to show the difficulty of arriving at a comprehension of psychic manifestations even from a relatively one-sided point of view, as has been done in this investigation of the libido, in which other aspects, such as Ego development, Super-Ego influence, defence mechanisms, etc., have purposely been omitted. Mental manifestations are so manifold and are the result of so many different tendencies—often contradictory—that even the limitation to a single principle of explanation, such as that of the theory of instinct, results in a complicated presentation. However, in order to gain a deeper insight into psychic material, Freud's theory of the libido has become indispensable. No adequate psychological approach is possible without it.

INDEX